Intervale

Intervale

New and Selected Poems

Betty Adcock

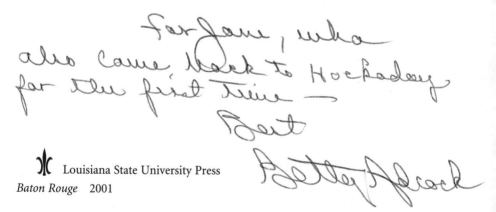

Louisiana State University Press

Baton Rouge 2001

Designer: Barbara Neely Bourgoyne
Typeface: Centaur and Minion
Typesetter: Coghill Composition, Inc.
Printer and binder: Thomson-Shore, Inc.

Library of Congress Cataloging-in-Publication Data

Adcock, Betty.
    Intervale : new and selected poems / Betty Adcock.
        p.   cm.
    ISBN 0-8071-2664-0 (cloth : alk. paper)
    I. Title.
    PS3551.D396 I58   2001
    811'.54—dc21   00-048553

Poems herein have been selected from *Walking Out* (Louisiana State University Press, 1975), *Nettles* (Louisiana State University Press, 1983); *Beholdings* (Louisiana State University Press, 1988); and *The Difficult Wheel* (Louisiana State University Press, 1995).

    Thanks to the editors of the following publications, in which some of the new poems, or versions of them, first appeared: *DoubleTake, Georgia Review, Gettysburg Review, Shenandoah, Southern Review, Tar River Poetry,* and *Vanderbilt Review.*

    "Digression on the Nuclear Age" and "Rent House" (from *Beholdings*) first appeared in *TriQuarterly,* a publication of Northwestern University.

    "Penumbra" was reprinted in *Pushcart Prize XXIV: Best of the Small Presses.* "Untitled Triptych" was commissioned by the North Carolina Museum of Art for *The Store of Joys: Writers Celebrate the North Carolina Museum of Art's Fiftieth Anniversary* (Blair Press, 1997).

    Thanks also to Meredith College for support, to Dabney Stuart for help, and to my husband, Don, for everything.

for my mother, Sylvia
for my daughter, Sylvia
and for my granddaughter, Tai

Contents

from *Beholdings* (1988)

from *The Difficult Wheel* (1995)

New Poems

PENUMBRA

The child in the cracked photograph sits still
in the rope swing hung from a live oak.
Her velvet dress brims with a lace frill.

Her pet Bantam is quiet in her lap.
It is the autumn day of a funeral
and someone has thought to take a snap-

shot of the child who won't be allowed
to go to the burying—the coffin in the house
for days, strange people going in and out.

She's dressed as if she'd go, in the blue church-
dress from last Christmas, almost too short.
The rooster loves her, she guards his perch

on her lap, his colors feathering the mild air.
She concentrates on this, now that her father
is unknowable, crying in his rocking chair.

Her mouth knife-thin, her small hands knotted hard
on the ropes she grips as if to be rescued.
She's growing a will that won't be shed

and something as cold as winter's breath
tightens in her, as later the asthma's vise
will tighten—hands on the throat, the truth.

Black and white, she is hiding
in every one of my bright beginnings.
Gold and deep blue and dark-shining

red the cockerel's feathers, gold the sun
in that skyblue southern fall, blue
over the four o'clocks and the drone

of weeping that drains like a shadow from the house
where someone is gone, is gone, is gone—
where the child will stay to darken like a bruise.

I am six years old, buried
in the colorless album.
My mother is dead.
I forgive no one.

INTERVALE

for my mother, Sylvia Hudgins Sharp, 1902–1944

At a distance, one hears voices that stray from the mark,
but in the center, in the midst of the terrific volume,
it is as if the imperfections are burned away.
   —Buell Cobb, Sacred Harp, A Tradition and Its Music

Forgive the song that falls so low
Beneath the gratitude I owe.
It means thy praise, however poor.
An angel's song can do no more.
   —The B. F. White Sacred Harp, 1902
      words by William Cowper, English poet, ca. 1779
      music by Oliver Holden, American carpenter

In pockets of the poor-white South,
in Primitive Baptist churches, pure delight
and grief in equal streams flowed straight
toward heaven, a preview of the crossing over
all would make. Workhorses, such churches
were plain-boarded, offering the simplest
backless benches to the sore afraid,
to the lonely and the praiseful come to sing.
Always one yellowjacket buzzed against
a rippled windowpane. Always the rough
grain of the walls held stories
children could guess at while the old songs broke
hard as a storm at sea above their heads.

First, *solmization,* the *fa-sol-la,*
notes in geometric shapes sung by their names
from the pages of that oddly oblong
Alabama book, and in modes closer
to the Greek than any since the Middle Ages.
Organum—oldest form of harmony—
is like this sound, living medieval

in the stripped-down Protestant
churches standing still in deep
East Texas woods.

After these fixed syllables have loosed
like glossolalia the music's tongues,
the words that follow might as well be dance.
Round after round of voices overlaid
repeat and contradict, death becomes light
and want is made like joy.
This is music deepening like a wound
bloodwelling,
and like a healing water poured.

The benches in a square, four parts
facing each other, no part subordinate—
in absolute democracy. This way
melody, nearly buried, is unearthly
tenor-carried, hardly heard
under waves of voices harsh as argument.
The beat drives hard as a worksong,
joyful as ringing stone from which a figure
rises as life under the hands of a master.
Words and music weave the fugue,
a skyward spiral, heavy stair
on which the Holy Spirit steps
clear and lightsome as a dove
into the world again.

Bass

The Hill of Zion yields
A thousand sacred sweets.

In the clearing hacked out of woods
that still range wild behind it,
Zion Hill Church sailed dingy-white,
slant as a lost glacier,

dragging its scallop of gravestones,
hem of the named dust—

What wondrous love is this.

Enforested, their voices shaped a strict
entablature on artless air,
a geometry of hope so pure it held
them truly out of harm, miraculous
as children saved in a windstorm's eye.
The beat surged like a running creature,
the heart's bare holy beast
barely contained. This song was raised,
already half a century late,
in the year my mother was born
and joined the communal
and lonesome local instrument,
brotherhood and sisterhood of breath
and no help for it.

Are there anybody there like Mary aweeping?

Here and now, summer heat
goes sidewise and upward,
visible and invisible together
in waver and blur—
and is like that confounding
ghost-music, stark harmony
with intervals so wide
a door's blown open in the world
for passage of the silenced
third, the sound of the missing,
which is God's.

TENOR

Just beyond this vale of sorrow
Lies the fields of endless day.

Town that never quite materialized:
Mt. Enterprise, where no mountain was,
where even the hill in the name
of the church was never more
than somebody's notion, and enterprise
laid itself early down in the splayed
shadow of the one grocery.
Here great-grandfather Will Hudgins
brought hard religion and nothing else
from Georgia after Sherman.
Here my mother grew: here she began,
with her multitude of kin, to sing.

How many years has man been driven
Far off from happiness and heaven?

Here she brought me in my fifth summer,
her last visit backward
from her teaching and our life elsewhere.
One year later, her sudden death would lift
her from me, and would take this place
out of my life completely as she was lost
in the open space of the world's
hard fugal turn, the soundless gate
that is simply sung
into the darkening firmament.

We lay our garments by
Upon our bed to rest.

On that one summer visit,
all that would be mine was laid down here
in memory, now shifty as groundfog.
Her parents' house held the solid, galvanized
aura of well water. I bathed cool and happy
in the big tin washtub on the porch,
raw beam and naked birdsong overhead.
Coal oil lamps sweated their too-warm light

with a strangely cold scent like a knife's.
There was a splintery woodpile, tendrils
of stovesmoke in the house, and a foreign
smell of coffee beans
parching in the iron oven.

My grandfather, big as a tree,
prayed, then drank his coffee black,
pouring it first into the saucer
where it trembled and cooled.
Their garments were laid by, years of them,
stitched into quilts made whimsical
with names: Log Cabin and Texas Star,
Wedding Ring and Crazy Patch—
piled to make my pallet on the floor,
whole countries of poverty's colors
I'd sleep across.

INTERLUDE: OTHER VOICES

VERA:

Your mother was my favorite sister.
She knew how to live, somehow,
even though we were so poor she had
just one dress her first year
to go to school.
Seems like anytime we moved out of a house,
it would start right then to fall down.
Sometimes it'd start before we left.
Papa made syrup, and we sold that. But cotton
was the real cash crop. For not much cash.
We farmed maybe fifty acres, sometimes less.
Papa was a carpenter too. One year he built
a man a house for the trade of thirty hogs.
That was going to be the year's money.
Every last one of those hogs died of cholera.
That was our kind of luck.

We all sang fa-sol-la at church.
And at home we sang. Papa found a thrown away
pump organ somewhere, and fixed it up.
He made himself a working fiddle out of pine.

A HOUSTON COUSIN:

When our grandmother was buried at Zion Hill,
the churchyard was empty when it was time to start.
I thought nobody had come.
Then, out of nowhere, they were there,
not coming from the road, not from cars—
and this was in the 1960s. They wore overalls,
some of the women in sunbonnets,
all that generation stepping quiet
from that wall of woods behind the church.
I tell you it scared me.
They walked right out of the trees.

A COUNTRY WOMAN:

Your mother taught me high school and I never
was one to love books, but the way she'd read
poems out loud like it was Bible
could make me just about hear music.
The words would stick right to me.

JIM:

She was the oldest of us nine
and raised us all. I was more scared
of her than I was of Papa,
she was that strict. And she could
pick more cotton than any of us boys,
more than a grown man, nearbout.
Because she just had to do the best
at anything she did. Anything.
She was about ten when Gene was born

and Mama said she could choose her brother's name.
She did: Eugene Field Hudgins
after somebody that wrote a poem.

MARY:

She pulled us up by her bootstraps
was what she did.

EVVA:

Get all the knowledge you can, she told me,
of literature and art.

VERA:

What did she like to do? Well, besides
visiting that library over at Baylor
after she was grown, I think it was
the simplest things. How can I say this—
she was just hooked on what most people
never notice in their lives because of work,
or not time enough.
She loved a common sunset, stars, ditchflowers,
lightning starting up, and anything rare
and lovely like the snow.
Right up until she died she'd walk in the woods
alone the way she did when we were kids,
gathering something maybe, hickory nuts
or branches of pretty leaves. But more than that.
I used to think she left us then completely,
though she'd be home all laden down
with something nice. I used to feel like
she was letting something go.

TREBLE

When we from time remove . . .

Yellow pine, sweet gum, live oak,
dogwood and sassafras

shadow the one-room school
where the girl my mother dreams
independence, transformation, travel
out of roughened fields that wait for her,
heat like a stone on her forehead,
chitter of insects.
A line of poetry flows through
the lesson she shares with her sister.
She will fish with that.
Later she'll hold the book just so
as she leans on an overgrown creekbank
behind the little farm,
will hold a clean, unspoken wish
like a spindle gathering
all that can clothe her life
with private joy:
words with a shine on them,
a run of minnows in the light.
Her half-Indian grandmother has touched
her cheekbones, has given her the thick black hair
that will early streak with silver.

Shall we know each other there?

If I dare rosebramble and snakes to find
where the hog pasture held on awhile,
past where the syrup mill was turned
by the one mule, past what was a broad field
of cotton my mother dragged her heavy sack across—
if I go deeper into penumbral timber
and find the creek where she sat down
to read poems, her feet in bright water,
what figure can I raise beyond
the glazed and flattened portrait
framed in all her family's regard?

Along what fault line might I,
had she lived, have measured and found myself?

COUNTER

Time, what an empty vapor 'tis.

Swallowing its tail,
time's hard fuguing tune
will send us worldless through
the opened door to death,
is mother to all form,
and is all formlessness.

We nail these octaves down
any way we can.

On those doomed polar expeditions
the nineteenth century so strenuously blessed,
weren't mammoths found
altogether present in the ice
like great stopped clocks?
Once I heard the story of an explorer
killed in a crevasse, and how his son,
a quarter of a century gone by,
came to that place and found the frozen father,
perfect and much younger than himself.

A sliver of cold is still part of my heart.
Look into the black space
where there was a house:
kettle rim, washtub rib, cotton-fleshed
quilt pattern, cold knuckle of washday,
ax head, pump handle, towsack,
the long bones of the lamplight—
what little I remember stares through pane
on pane the present turns opaque.

What figure can I raise?

POSTLUDE

And if there is no figure, only light?

Alone in the rich house of my father's people,
I dreamed this place, the strange girl my mother,

my own buried life. It is my wish, my fever
I've come here to discover by slow-moving
water loosing three pure notes, almost cool.
And nothing is so clear.
Like melting ice, the glass
flows out of the picture frame—
my face, my own reflection.

Across the forest canopy, bright with birds,
a small wind starts to hum
first notes of the hymn,
wide breath all breath becomes.
That tune is gapped and partial,
rough, modal, unkind to the ear,
fugue entwining loss and praise
no less than in the doubled
helixes that sing the living world.

LOCOMOTION

Perhaps a woman could leave this, grown
finally past her father's house.
Perhaps she could learn again.
But the door's black frame
leads into another, house
after house. Her life
is put together like a train.

For whole moments between, the sun
pours and the trees proffer bright leaves,
though none of this, nor thrush song,
nor the simple wheel of blue air briefly
over her can hold. She moves,
possession after possession, into the next

oblong of darkness. She is no longer
able to guess what engine tows,
what follows close.
Whole time zones flare and pass.
Something we love is out there—
where among the passing fields?

Is there not in each of us
one scene, one moment that comes back
as if our lives moved only to bring us there,
to that weather and that landscape where we grasped
the one thing we would carry over?
It might be nothing but a sunstruck creekbank,
a yellow bird, a ditch of flowers.

It is an orchard. Its peaches soften
near a rolling pasture where cattle
are fixed as ritual, mist at their knees,
fruited air harboring a light intending

to be music, bees at their devotions,
the sky a clean blue.

On the day she sees it flickering beside her,
she'll slam her white hand through
that landscape snared in window glass,
a smell of summer bursting from her fingers,
summer burning with a sudden rain.

She'll reach for fragments,
broken amber holding what's at once
ancient and larval.
Her hands grow rich with imaginings,
brilliant with splinters, words, arrival.

FINAL CUT

The 1940s: my father's hat
is rakish, cocky, the way men
wore hats then, though he is sad,
is lost. I have to find him.

And my mother: ghostface
drifting anchorless in the deepened
dream I'm flailing through at dawn—
the mother dead now fifty years
and I'm the child still fishing for the body.
Not much to go on.

Grandparents: their ripe and beasty world,
the cows and goats, the corn, the melon field.
Find the two people in this picture,
quiet as grazing stock,
green as the fruiting stalks.

Here's a photograph of children: my father
and his sisters with their pony, with
slingshots and stiff, makeshift dolls.
Always there are dogs in these pictures
brown with sunspots.

The only child of this, and late,
I am the last reel, the fate
of this song and dance, the final spool
on which they whirl.

I work hard to get it right—camera, lights—
crank up a day in brown with sunspots,
antique cars coughing into life, dogs
forlorn, adrift, that hat holding its tilt;
faces in the fadeout fading back.

The future is the part I cannot get.

And soon enough the whole thing will shut down—
vowel, cadence, image, rhyme—
like an album closing. Some intelligent machine
is taking itself off-line.
This must be the reason
the brown dogs are frantic, the cars careening,
cornstalks ballooning, sunspots chasing
my father's hat that is rolling hugely
down the Keystone sepia street.
This must be the accident about to happen.

No one is in the theater to clap.

Perhaps I'm walking under a yellow sun outside,
such brightness as comes into the world
after the story. See the shadows vanish
into reconstructed scenery that vanishes
with its picnics and parades and funerals
like leather volumes with old letters tucked inside.
I'm feeling how light I will be, happy
as a creature off its leash,
blear-eyed, indifferent, perfectly blank.

I've been given some sort of award.
There's no one here to thank.

SUMMER

Roomful of early evening, airy curtains plying
a slant wind along the open-windowed wall,
the screens x-ing a veil on leaves dusk-dampened,
cicadas, birds at raucous vespers calling back

another house: day's end, the steep backsteps
where I'd sit, a child watching the world fade,
loving the way the hens called out and then flew up
into the shadowy crepe myrtle. Each plump bundle
landed with a thump on a chosen branch
to chortle, then chuckle, then tick,
ruffling and settling among the chewed-pink
blossoms into unsteady sleep.

Another July—ten o'clock and dead dark—
my grandfather rocked on the deep front porch,
a box of heat no breeze could quite cut through,
his cigarette an outsized firefly
brightening and softening, staying
while the tiny lanterns in the yard
burned on and off, high and higher
in the trees until they stopped.
Sometimes, laying fireglow on the porch-edge,
he'd cup his hands and blow an owl's call,
moon-shaped, like a kiss.
That's an old horn-owl, he'd say. *Now listen.*
And the owl's answer floated back, an echo
of an echo—one absolutely perfect thing repeating—
like feathers, like clouds, like the heat itself
out loud in fathoms of darkness.

And when I was sixteen, in my twilit room upstairs
I tied and retied the shining shoulder-straps
of a new red polished-cotton dress
with rhinestones on the bodice.

The heat licked all the powder off my face.
My stockings stuck. The crinoline slip wilted.
Only my red-polished lips stayed perfect
while I waited for the crunch of tires, waited
every sweltering Saturday night
for the boy's light step on the porch.
We'd hit every roadhouse that had a dance floor
between home and Louisiana. Hollis could dance
better than anyone—he taught me, that chancy summer,
every single step I'd ever need
to keep the backroads and the jukeboxes alive.

Four years older and much surer than I,
he vanished into September, gone to the army,
and I neither heard from him nor much cared,
having begun myself
the long mystery of leaving, my solitary run.
Now in this room among Carolina trees,
in my good life that can sometimes feel
tentative after forty years,
one solstice dusk unscrolls those hens
rustling and crooning in the winey myrtle,
my grandfather's owl-voice opening the night,
that dress like a red reflection, my hot face—

and the way the future fluttered soft and mothlike,
unnoticed against dark glass that separated
what was from what was *not yet.*
Now that message ricochets
from memory to here: Hollis blew out
his heart with a shotgun three years after
we shagged across rough county lines and laughed.
Dance-time and echo. Summer. Feathers and fire.

INLAND HURRICANE

It's hard to talk about. Nightlong noise,
hellwind that lasted hours, the tossed toys
our trees became—there aren't words
for that savage dervishing of rain and air,
or for the way we felt, the dreadful ache
a concrete floor sends banging through the bones
as if the din outside came deeply in
to stay. We heard some of the house come down.
Which part? It was all guessing until dawn.

The poor cat sped from window to black
basement window, chasing the strange scent
thickening the world like something live.
How to describe it: it was singed spores,
a fire that wasn't burning, a flood that was.
The cat like a bowstring answered
whatever out there belled the wind.
It was all warning and nothing, nothing to be done.

When we finally entered sleep, like falling ill,
it was no darker there.
At daybreak, we came upstairs like swimmers rising.
The house was whole, except for our bedroom
the largest oak took down.
It was the landscape that had gone.

From world awash in light that was
both bright and dismal, with a warmth in it
like blood or semen, stifling.
No birds were out.
The stintless hum that marks our days,
machine hum we hardly hear and can't
hear silence for, had disappeared.

The house felt full, as if a pressure
built inside had stayed, a restlessness

like a soul that couldn't go.
At every window, the branches of downed trees
were splayed against glass,
staining the light—every single room
was garrisoned with green.

Something had changed. A profound derangement lived
even in our bodies, something intelligent
and still and most absurdly new, a beauty
poised as if to leap toward more of itself—
death as possibility. It was the old
feral emptiness before our world was made.

TO A BRILLIANT YOUNG PROFESSOR
WHOSE CANCER IS INOPERABLE

On a ledge that only the young
who are dying are forced to inhabit,
you hold out, the shining gone
that was a stifled lamp in your father's
ignorant house, in your mother's eyes.
Changeling, you came up wayward
out of the ritual furrows, wild
for knowledge and the world.

Now you look back straight
as the row was plowed, forgetting the curse
you felt when the whole congregation
prayed out loud in the clapboard church
for your soul on the smothering September night
before you fled to the suspect university.
You told us how the moth-winged heat bore down
on fumbling hymns, on the rage you fidgeted
through in silence, hounded
by blank faith you had already shed.
Their faces were lined up, you said,
dull as a row of pans.
You had dared to set
the fathers' teeth on edge.

Dressed as your shadow now, you've turned
like a plowhorse. Bright years behind, ahead,
drift away as dust in a field.
You've grasped the slack hands of a preacher
who promises with his one book to keep you.

No one can keep you.

But friends and lovers, distanced now,
may someday stand where you are standing

stilled. Anyone, anyone may unearth the will
to bargain back the tribal hearth,
the oldest cave, shades of whatever story
can color bare original walls of stone
with hope, with fabulous continuance.
For now, we watch from far off, unable
to follow where you crouch beside that fire—
ignis fatuus to us, ignoble, strange.
But you, lit with deliverance,
are beautiful and dear, at home at least
until the mortal dumb-show ceases
or is changed.

LATE SNOW, LATE CENTURY

Our old pear tree had flowered, early lace,
when this mild winter turned to bite its tail.
Heavy and delicate, the tree is twice
lovely with the sky's cast bloom, twice pale.

Does flowering lead the metaphor? Or what is borne
by flowering? Radiant opposites touch and burn:
so Leda must have held the blinding swan.
Which glory fountained upward, which rained down?

Later, we'll thirst against a towering light
that shines alone and burnishes no fruit.

PILGRIMAGE

to Don, who came back to me first in Greek, and then entirely

1   PAST TENSE

Where did you go in your almost-leaving,
that emptied, antiseptic hesitation
in which your body, icicle-still, was fastened
to a console like a spaceship's? In what room
of the world did you countenance
three blank days?
                              All of us saw
it was deeper than sleep, the place
you faced bluntly into, becoming silence
carved into likeness.

The grim foretaste: our fast
twilight drive in muddy air, the harried
dense gray of the hospital parking lot.
Refusing a wheelchair, you limped in,
pain in your back like a bayonet.
It was midnight before they discovered
the three layers of your aorta's wall
were coming apart like wet cardboard.

2   RELIVING

Empty at 3 A.M., the waiting room
lengthens before me like a road.
No one sits at the desk where the telephone
crouches. No one calls a name.
The lights are off: a single shaft
opens one small door just enough
to spread a deep-wool dusk
across the long room, long hours
I try to remember how to pray—
just enough

to let a sliver of paradise, unbidden, enter
my eye. It is that perfect April light
we found in Greece, unwintering
the world, weaving and reweaving the Aegean
blue and again and again blue.

From this dull room, muffled green walls
and mirroring windows backed with night,
I send you memory more workable than prayer.
I send you Siphnos, island in blossom,
and our village, Katavati, its wandering streets
thrumming with the small hooves of donkeys,
its very air alive and singing,
astringent with wild thyme,
vehement with bees.

I might be a telegrapher at this task,
tapping out the *azure* and *cinnabar*
of new-painted doors and the *bride-white*
of light-washed houses, tapping out
garlic-sharpened scent of lamb on a spit,
the shine of fish in a red net, the intense
speech of the lemon tree in sunlit declensions.

Across the hospital's linoleum, across shadows
of empty chairs and the distant *whisk*
of elevator doors, I send you the one moment
when every olive tree on the terraced mountain
turns silver in the quickened wind.

Come with me out of that room
where metal and white tile are adamant
in freezing light, where men wearing masks
have sawed through the stronghold and opened
your ribs, have taken and lifted
your live heart in their hands as if it were
a red mullet to be thrown to shore.

Oh come with me
up the hundred whitewashed steps
from the sea to the defunct monastery
whose church still holds its miracle-
working Virgin. Fretted in silver, she
is wrapped in white cloth and new ribbons
for April procession. Just so,
Athena was each year newly clothed.
Nothing is changed but names in this world.

The churchyard is tumbled with wind-ridden roses,
the antique kind whose thick perfume can stun,
whose colors are so beautifully unreliable.
I would take you even to the mountain cemetery
with its sentinel cedars and jumble of stones,
each with a glassed-in portrait
and a lamp kept always full.
I have burned such inexhaustible oil
all night before a thing that is not God
but may be the hem of His garment,
which to touch is to be made whole.

I have walked again and again
to the hospital's chapel, unable
to stay there, unable to be anywhere
but in this deadly room,
on the couch whose dimming pattern
has absorbed the sweat of the terrified,
the soon-to-be-grieving.
In this odd boat I have traveled,
rocked by wave-slap and dread,
to the island we loved together,
and I have brought it whole, rose and rockface,
icon and almond tree, star by vivid star.
I have sent it like a skimming stone
across these miles of shined floors,
fluorescent corridors, thin air.

3 QUESTION AND ANSWER

On the fourth day you could begin
to breathe alone, but speech wouldn't come—
a stroke brought on by surgery.
What grace or luck had made it mild?

For days you strained toward
ordinary words.
It would be weeks before the brain
stopped reeling.
     How was it, then,
that you spoke to me in your first
thin consciousness, still unable to move?
And clearly: *Kala. Kala, efkaristo!*
As we had spoken thanks on the island
after a dance, a loaf, a piece of lamb
was given,
    and the music had again begun.

MAKING

I thought I was moving on
but all of us are rooted like child labor
to something assigned, humming
like bees. We don't, of course, know why
or even how we work.

All those long days, years,
the fast version of things
slips through the fingers, smooth,
clear patterns tumbling from rattling looms:
grandmothers, babies, wars, soup,
hickory nuts and wet leaves, whole towns,
crowds of faces, close calls, love's hot
start and the rush to begin again.
All this time it's been running,
the fabric beginning to thin, coursing
more like thought than like material
until it thickens once, a selvage, done.
Then we are freed of all design.

By then, the wind, shroudmaker,
can carry all I am.
I may sing across stones, drift
over the blue domes and white houses
of one small Greek island forever,
foreign and perfectly at home.
Memory weighs nothing. Our intricate
finished product
can vanish into light.

EVOLUTIONS

> the Karakaroms, or Black Gravel Range: mountains
> on the border between Pakistan and China

Here is birthplace: vivid line
where Asia and subcontinent met
in unimaginable collision. That

was seventy million years ago,
and still this land is never
still; the very ground
still in the making shakes,
unsettled as a tapestry
some giant Penelope unmakes.
Earthquakes happen daily here,
and glaciers wander an easy span
of several football fields between
sunrise and the rising moon.

In the Karakaroms, nothing yet is
(or everything is) quite past,
and what turns up
                                inclines to last:
cold, and motion, the slow molting
of ice, the loud manufacture of mountains.

People, on the other hand,
do what we can:
as you'll have guessed,
there is a road of sorts.
There are some settlements.
and *élan vital* to excess

when planes from Air Force Pakistan
bomb glaciers to protect a town.
Fire and ice together then.

Hot war? Cold War? Culture? Nature?
We lack a proper nomenclature
for this event horizon where
after's the same thing as *before*.

DECEMBER

A sky all smoke and winter glimmer
in the trees. I could imagine
those trees. But they are these,
far out of summer though summer's rag-ends
tremble, manage a faint resplendence
in the sun that's left,
that's leaving now, that's almost
set, small dazzles hidden in the weather.
It's as if a muffled, humable tune
turned suddenly modal, different but known.

It takes me,
this backyard we bought the house for,
back. Sweet gum, maple, hickory, oak
and one rare sentinel hemlock keeping
by the creek its patch of shadow—
half acre of trees that can seem to widen,
become the whole farm climbing
that hill where a grove embraced
the old house beloved and broken
out of. At what cost? I can't remember
And now missed? Yes and never.
I was aiming elsewhere. Here,

winter mists bloom in the branches,
A trainwhistle ribbons its shining
steelblue cry, diminishing, then gone.
Sometimes that sound, or an owl's ritual
call riding the night like a low cloud,
will wake me to cold dark
when something is targeted, something . . .
just then one perfect shriek will speak
for the torn, or silence for the lost.

Then again—long-voweled, sundered—
one of the ways of traveling will sing
among shadowless trees, memory
or future, low on the changeful wind.

RENOVATED ZOO, NOW CALLED *HABITAT*

This is their better life, each kind in place
where low walls and cunning moats address
an almost beautiful, almost spacious,
almost accurate wilderness.

Now the lion's breath can feather
great clouds on a larger winter;
the wolf trot longer as he burns
his pattern on this lengthened run;
and we see more of the lustrous otter's
turning into underwater's
sudden turning into glass.

Here's envisioned jungle and savanna,
mirages verging on suburban
where the aging leopard lunges,
and elephants, our lapsing emblems
of the Pleistocene's parade,
in thunder-colored skins go under
imported trees, allotted shade.

On the tiger passant, light and dark engage
to adumbrate an antique cage.
Forward and back, and back, and back,
his roiling stride of silk and rage
mocks the old constricting track.

What comes here after dark? Not ease.
Perhaps the city's nightmare comes
to each of these, and shaped as they are shaped:
clawed fierce-footed if that is right,
beaked and flying if it flies,
or coiled and striking, saffron eyed—
our fantasy assailing as our manufacture takes
them into art and absence and desire.

ELLA RICHARD

born 1875, buried 1953

Grandmother, I need you,
your time like a hood, your houseful.
From the parlor's corners, dust would dance
constellations visible in window-narrowed sun.
The furniture so heavy it was never moved
cast outsized shadows, faintly animal,
nailing down the afternoons.
Late, from porch chairs in the dark,
the moon we saw was yours. Like you,
it went thinner.
Like you, it came back.

Your fingers stained with dewberries
(kitchen full of glass, the boiling purple),
your scissors shaped like a tiny stork
(white china darning egg in the basket),
the lace you tatted with a bone hook—
In my daydream your hands are browsing
brittle pages of the huge *Book of Birds,*
parsing colors, plumages that told
foreign places, another way of things.
That unadventurous liking for the world
never took you farther than the mockingbird
playacting in the yard.
You'd say to me, *We'll just step round*
and pick some of that yellowbell by the lane.
You meant the winding wider-than-a-path that barely
got itself to the road, your words for it
and the blooming bush
already a small allegiance.

In your twenties you were
Woman at the Turn of the Century.

How grand it sounds—
you could be a textbook!
We write poems that pretend we're you,
our words in your mouth—the taste
would shrivel your tongue like green persimmons.

The story we tell is full of props, of course,
but just as full of truth. It's just
that there's more to it than we say,
more than the vote you got but never used,
more even than that purest truth
you told your three grown children:
If I'd known how not to,
I'd never have had a one of you.
You said it without anger or despair.
It was simply there, as they were,
your loved children grown, to whom
you owed no more than the late care
of saying things out plain.

And now we are the moon's
long, clear fingers practicing our reach.
We think there's more to know our shining for.
There is.
              And still we need your
ordinary birds, those migrations now
more certain on a yellowed page
than in our air.
              We need, for light,
the presences of bone and lace, wild berries,
eggs of milky glass, a flowering of old names,
and scissors sharp and cunning-shaped for luck.
None of us would live again your losses
but who among us would not choose,
sometimes, such plain necessities,
path that was simply there, winding toward
what gathered on the world like fruit,
and each thing with its shadow-opposite
not spoken of, but known.

FOR TAI LANE RUINSKY, GRANDDAUGHTER

written on the eve of her arrival from China, age
seven months, in celebration of her adoption

You will come to us with the other
landscape in your eyes, your hands still
cupped around the air of Jiang Xi.
Like any beginning, you will wear
paradox—solemnity and dazzle,
sunsparks on sober distances
of the River Gan.
Behind you the years in their thousands
are massed, murmuring like boats
poled across heavy water.

Your mother has fashioned a shining
nursery. There, under the yellow quilt
printed with gentled animals,
you will go on traveling awhile,
taking your time at arrival.
In your throat, you hold the first stirrings
of an ancient dialect; in your ears
a sound of bells like audible mist
that will fade

          or stay only
in dreams once the American light
enters you, that light lovely as summer
on the best field, and foolish with plenty.
You come from a poor village of the south,
a province famous for porcelain
and peasant uprisings. You will keep
the color red for good fortune,
for the spilled blood of your ancestors,
here where the story of freedom and failure

is dangerous too, chiaroscuro
with its own red source.

For now, we wait with our burdens,
offering ourselves, our intractable histories.
From your father: Eastern Europe and
the lost—whole populations of smoke—
and the immigrant prayers of the tailor
from Russia, the tailor from Poland.
From your mother, from her father and me,
all the American contradictions:
slaveholders, dirt farmers, factory workers,
teachers, deserters, one carpenter-preacher,
one herbalist-midwife.

When your voice begins to build
our words, when your hands begin
to grasp our hands,
our images replacing shadowy faces,
your mother will be singing to you
the songs I sang to her. Your father
will remember all the games of his childhood.

We will graft your river to our river,
numberless tributaries! We will live
on one bank of that mystery.
So many boats are stilled in the harbor;
see how they join to make the bridge
on which you, child,
will cross and recross, dancing
this difficult story.

CYCLADIC FIGURE

*Better than Brancusi. Nobody has ever made an
object stripped that bare.*
   —Picasso

After the Fall,
after the plummet from pliable green
and lambent shadow, all impression
of the garden vanished. Imprints
of blossom and fruit, entangling vine,
leaf and animal and bird
in their once and perfect forms—
these have been excised.
Exile has pared this image;
implement and need have come.

And the mild, vaporous dawn
that could not die is lost.
Lost, the life on which wild world
engraved itself, blunt kinship
with beasts and stars in that *before*
where bloodshed daily was
unconscious and undone.

Not yet begun: the known,
our waking dream, labor of time
and the mistaking mind.
Soft Minoan frescoes are not quite
imagined. Inconceivable the Attic
art that will be born in grace
and die diffused in ornament.
Languages, philosophies to be caught
in the nets of possibility, faiths
and wars and kingdoms—none is yet.

Luminous, seeming to be made purely
of tenuous light, this figure clasping its own

form is born altogether of earth
that has given such reflection
again into our hands,
a charm, a grave conjecture
thin as the new moon.

This candle we may bear
as we have done before
into the sepulcher.

JANUARY

Dusk and snow this hour
in argument have settled
nothing. Light persists,
and darkness. If a star
shines now, that shine is
swallowed and given back
doubled, grounded bright.
The timid angels flailed
by passing children lift
in a whitening wind
toward night. What plays
beyond the window plays
as water might, all parts
making cold digress.
Beneath iced bush and eave,
the small banked fires of birds
at rest lend absences
to seeming absence. Truth
is, nothing at all is missing.
Wind hisses and one shadow
sways where a window's lampglow
has added something. The rest
is dark and light together tolled
against the boundary-riven
houses. Against our lives,
the stunning wholeness of the world.

UNTITLED TRIPTYCH

Anselm Kiefer
German, born 1945

Untitled, 1980–86

Oil, acrylic, emulsion, shellac, lead,
charcoal and straw mounted on
photograph mounted on canvas, with
stones and lead and steel additions.

Overall: 130⅝ × 222¼ in.

North Carolina Museum of Art
Purchased with funds from the State of
North Carolina, W. R. Valentiner, and
various donors, by exchange
94.3 © Anselm Kiefer

Photograph courtesy North Carolina
Museum of Art

UNTITLED TRIPTYCH

Anselm Kiefer, German, born 1945

Left Panel

The leaden landscape is itself a twilight
shadowing these massive rocks, the severed
puppet-strings of heaven dangling
like electric wires. The great stones drop
out of no sky.

                  Or these lines are the broken
cables of gravity that braided
granite to earth, iron to earth,
cut now like balloon-strings.
Distracted boulders rise
in graceless desire without
any color on them of light,
adamantine in the pure
negatives of fire: slag, ashes—
the smelter's children
rising as the first mountains
rose on pinions of stone.

There can be no horizon.

Right Panel

Here is a country in which fire has eaten,
in which the storm opens its mouth.
Flecks of lead flare half-hidden,
engine-glints among great patches of lichen
or rot, as if ruins long asleep
had waked.

                  Or these are patches of bombsmoke
graying huge distances, small bits of metal

descending, a confetti of shrapnel or
starshine. A mockery of rain
falls toward a mockery of bloom:
one tumorous blossom reaching out
on its corkscrewing stem—
the root upgrown or
the tornado touching down.

             And this is also the mangled
loudspeaker, sorcerer's vortex
into which the detritus of war has drained:
teeth, shoes, the light-bitten bone.
Out of such dark cornucopias
the voices marched in trick fire,
language of ashes taking the names.

             If it be as well
the alchemist's funnel, breakable
vessel encoded as spirit,

what is here transformed?

CENTER PANEL

             It is possible not to see
the serpent.
Light would break around it but cannot,
is reined into the thing itself:
helix of intermittent
lumps of light and coal-chunks of shadow—
a boiling certainty in its cauldron of elements.
             It is possible not to see
the serpent. It is possible not to know if it is made
at all, of light or of darkness.

Overhead a damaged ladder launches
twelve steps toward heaven, twelve
toward the ground.

Or perhaps reflected light
scales only a piece of scalded railroad track
uplifted, no longer directed toward what was never
made in the alchemist's furnace: death
coining jewelry, tooth fillings, shoe leather, hair.
                                    Rung by rung this wounded
Jacob's ladder recites a desperate alphabet
depending from what may be
the flowering and serpent-making rod of Aaron—
                                    or may be only our blunt
iron inheritance:
the extruded industrial mind.

What reaches toward this narrowed, high
horizon? What climbs earthward
toward that cold fire?
Something is on its way to the sun.
Something is on its way out of the lightened sky.
A brightening almost golden
swirls in the thickening river,
eddies around the ladder.

                    Everything is awake here:
the promise of knowledge, which was death;
the promise of war, which is kept;
the promise of change, which keeps us.

This serpent is not trodden upon,
this thing only beginning
again as it has always begun,
though the bombs fell and the children
fell, and the gods fell in the fields,
as the world fell and keeps falling
out of the blank sky to become itself—
a mutable beauty, and terrible,
climbing like hope

out of the one coiled heart.

from Walking Out (1975)

AT THE FAIR

Before even the glorious ferris wheel,
we wanted the animals. "Wild!
Exotic!" yelled the menagerie man.
Inside, we watched the molting hawk ignore,
for the third year in a row,
boys and their sticks. The fox
caressed his cage door with a furious muzzle.
He was new, unused to noise.
We counted splinters in his nose.
The giant bat uncloaked himself, a mouse-mouthed yawn
and wing-tips touching wire on either side.
One old wildcat stalked his shadow
while his eyes stood still.
When we had seen them all,
we moved to the music and wheeling lights
where people were passing each other.
Behind each fixed look something quick walked,
jerked at the end of its chain, turned
to cross a face again.

VEGETARIAN

I step inside their circle,
boundaries of beanrows, my friends
with their gestures of cornstalks.
I sit at their green tables
where salt stains the plain fare
in spite of us, bad water
at the cabbage root.
Even the seeds smell of cold sweat.
Brown children are crying in the rice kernels.
Afraid of what we are, we try
for the innocence of straw.
Burst huts in Asia scatter
a throw of bones, fire-gnawed.
We are sleeping for another dream,
hoping to wake toothless,
wise.

1969

SISTER, THAT MAN DON'T HAVE THE STING OF A HORSEFLY

However, woman can never be a poet. She is a muse or
she is nothing.
    —Robert Graves, *The White Goddess*

But doubling's a speciality among us.
She looks from my mirror, that other's
face nobody suspects me of.

Part of the light in my eyes,
blind Texas sun I grew under, color
of brass, her face is loud as a street band
and as flat. I know how it feels
standing behind the "Eat-Here" counter in the bus station,
still as flypaper, waiting for the next one.
She's that kind of weather, never
taking no and never going far,
lighting up one after another.

The bastards don't bother her,
wanting that brassy light she's got,
wishing she'd get out of theirs or at least
take one of them home before she marries a plumber.
Years she's been mopping up
after babies and truck drivers.
Nothing they say surprises her.

ELIZABETH, CORNERED

Out of this
who can dance?
The spinster aunt knits my brow.
I remember the churchwindow
shedding saints' color like flaking paint.
I remember the grass face of my mother,
the stone she wore.

Once I dropped a live egg in the hen-roost,
watched the chick-sack's muffled beat.
I remember the fear of kisses, a shape
that still grows on ceilings.

Expose a pathos of breast and thigh
to the horned light?
To turn toad is better,
sitting a long time with rusty skin.

I saw a man who was made of birds.
He flew, a little at a time.
Oh the winged finger, the light elbow,
the lifted belly.

In the splayed house under my ribs,
I sit large and still as a portrait.
Who'd have thought the world thrown at me
out of God's angry fit could so have missed?

FOR SYLVIA, EIGHT YEARS OLD

In a wrung season, she hears the twig
touching its cold elbow, the wing
opening south, the water hiding
in the deep hands of the ice.

She answers the small doors:
worm, snail, the beetle prisoner
on his upended curve.

There, there the moth unfolds.
There the air parts for a feather.
She knows the wind's turn in the dust
and the steps of the rain.

For her the squirrel arches, and the bird
completes his invisible tower. For her
the cocoon's pulse keeps, and the web
stands in its two anchors.

Cornered in her eyes, the bright world
trembles unspilled, and love
like the wind in her long hair
is long enough.

FANTASY AT A POETRY READING

Tonight the bear is given his weight in meaning.
An elk wears flowers in his antlers. He'd eat them
if he could reach them.
The wolf is received as a brother. No one asks
if he'd rather be an only child.

A few Indians have been arranged for,
solemn as caterers.

Suddenly some unworded animal
steps live out of shreds of poems
and the room fills with the scent
of the utterly separate.
Poets fold inward like struck tents.
The creature (an otter? a badger?)
walks across them, leaving
delicate prints no one can read.

LOOKING FOR THE UNINVITED

You didn't come because you weren't called.
Not even a whistle in the dark
or a slippery accident
reached you. It can't
be said even that you wait.

Unhanded, in the only perfect freedom,
you are forever the day after.
What shape would you have given to this day,
a ripe plum, an hourful of grass and dandelions?
Even the dead can do that.

What shape would you have taken,
you with the millions of possible noses?
Nothing can own what you own,
no one, jack of all minds in my trade,
unlived son.

FOUR SHORT POEMS

1   AFTER THE VISIT

Friend of so many years
(at fifteen we wept together because Jesus
wasn't a thing to believe in anymore and because
we were afraid of sex and death and Latin),
it was good to see you again.
How is it that I am thriving, too plump
on nothing a month and very nearly
the same old fearful questions?
You are so sad, so thin,
nervously smoking in a rich house,
having seen the world and found Zen.

2   HALL MIRROR

Half ruined with age, it held
my clear child's face halved
by a botched future, impossible
dim old woman.

Now in the same glass
that child's eye is the dark one,
her mouth desperate as the bad half
of the witch's apple. Clearly the other
smiles, an eye of laughter.
The old woman knows what she's doing.

Everything changes sides.

3   ANSWERING THE PSYCHOANALYST

The long-legged living goes on
in thatched rooftops beneath this time,
in our sleep where the house is always
early and part of the earth.

Stork wings in updrafts of the blood,
red legs meadowing in the sun of our darkness,
from deep migrations they bring their legends,
their language of blows.

And we wear stories woven in rooftrees
the way our faces wear firelight, the way
our eyes wear blue chill at dawn.

Nests of strong thorns are gathered
to rock ghosts, those white eggs,
the luck.

4   GIFT

My father loved my mother when she died.
After that he stayed away from houses.
He lived with the running of the hounds and foxes
who made an old fierce grief articulate.

I learn still from small animals of wood
he carved and put into my hands instead of words.

SOUTHBOUND

You can go back in a clap of blue metal
tracked by stewardesses with drinks and virginal masks.
These will work whether you breathe or not. And this
is the first part. The way is farther
into thin roads that sway with the country.
Through the shine of a rented car the red towns rise
and crumble, leaving faces stuck to you like dust.
Following the farms, houses the color of old women,
you gather a cargo from yards full of lapsed
appliances, tin cans, crockery, snapped wheels,
weedy, bottomless chairs. These float through the air
to rest on the sleek hood, the clean seats.
Things broken out of their forms
move to you, their owner, their own.
You slow under weight. The windshield blurs
with the wingbeat of chickens. The hound's
voice takes over your horn.
A green glass vase from a grave in a field
comes flowerless to your hand, holds a smell
of struck matches, of summer on rust, of running
water, of rabbits, of home.

Then the one place flung up like a barrier,
the place where you stop, the last
courthouse and gathering of garrulous stores.
You have brought the town.
It walks in your skin like a visitor.
Here, under the wooden tongue of the church,
by the paths with their toothed gates,
in the light of the drunk as he burns
past hunkered children reaching
for the eyes of their fathers, these fading
and coming like seasons,
you are the tall rooms of your dead.

Merchants still ring small furious bells
and the window of the moviehouse opens,
and the girls who will, open.
Men still stand jackknifed to trace
deer trails in the dirt.
And blacks scythe the lawns, not singing,
keeping their flag hidden.

You may house again these weathers worn thin
as coins that won't spend, worn smooth
as the years between two who are old
and not fooled any longer. You may stand
beneath the café's blue sign where it steps
on the face like a fly. You may bend
to finger the cracked sidewalk,
the shape of stilled lightning, every fork
the same as it was when you thought that map
led to the rim of the world.

You may listen for thunder.

THINGS LEFT STANDING

That summer I trailed the creek
every day, daring to come
to the end of what I knew
with thin August water beside me,
the sun on the fields almost audible.

The last day, I turned with the creek
where a pine grove I had never seen
held a ruined country school, gutted
not by fire but by children
grown tall and permitted
their will among the unused.

In a coat of shadow and dead paint,
the walls seemed to fade, leaving outlines,
leaving one intact pane of glass
where the sun struck and gathered a shape
like the towhead of a child,
one who was left or whose ghost stayed
to study the seasons of corn.

Drawn in through a doorway of splinters,
I touched broken desks, touched
the smell of wasps, housedust, pine needles.
The back wall was gone,
the room left open and legible.
Names were cut deep in three walls,
and shapes: every sexual part, all things
male and female carved outsized,
whole new animals
in a wooden impossible book.

In the movement of shadow, that place
trembled with ritual, with the finding
that always is personless.

I spoke to the fields
severed names, fragments, forbidden
words notched crookedly, correct.

I lay down near a tree, slept,
and my dream shaped a man,
made simply of summer and grass,
who would take on a face, who would hold me
speaking the tongue of the touched.
I woke with the grass on my dress,
sharp stain that would stay.
The ghost that clouds any window
only at one angle of vision
was gone when I turned for home.

That which is given once
or thrown like a curse of a weapon
came both ways in the ruins of August.
I knew the dead child in the glass,
knew the sun with its open knife,
and I stood up in the smell of the future
to wear, as time had given,
green, deep scars of the light.

WALKING OUT

Fishing alone in a frail boat
he leaned too far, lost hold,
was turned out of the caulked world.
Seventy years he had lived without learning
how surfaces keep the swimmer up.

In that green fall, the churn of fear
slowing to pavane,
one breath held precious and broken,
he counted oar-strokes backward:
shore was not far.
This coin he took from the pocket of terror.

Starting over, over his head,
he reached for the earth.
As creatures of water once called on the future
locked in their bodies, he called on his past.
He walked. Walked. And there was enough
time, just enough, and luck.
Touching greenfingered sand, rising and touching,
body bursting with useless knowledge,
he came at the world from its other direction
and came to his place in air.

Back in his life now, he measures
distances one breath long,
talks less, flexes
the oars of his legs.

> Things shimmer where he is,
> his house, his earthcolored wife and sons.
> Every place raises walls around him
> the color of old glass.
> Heaven is a high clear skin.

Beneath the drift of flesh his bones remember
trying for bottom.

THE SIXTH DAY

Here where the river is naming itself
in heat that clings like a history,
two men walk with their knowledge of snakes,
the dance of the hunter, though their step
is arthritic now, altered.

One is my father. He has come
to fish with his oldest companion.
And this is not the place, but near it,
near the thick woods, net of beasts
these men have lived in as one might
stay on in a treacherous house
because it is home.

They will sit out an afternoon's sweat
to salt the river with stories
of guns with second sight, hounds
with the gift of speech,
deaths that struck back.

It is like the way they run fingers
over the sharp dust of antlers and boars' jaws
and the head of a wildcat my father
has nailed in his barn.
They talk and the thickets tangle
around them. Their compasses
break. They come again upon phosphorus
in the deadwood of midnight, brighter than foxes.

The two men have drawn up a few fish.
The day runs them down, a dragonfly
dimming on water. They rise
for their homes in that light.
And the red wolf is not here
nor the bear nor the wildcat

whose head on the wall is not magic enough
to raise the dead.

The two men are leaving
without eyes in the backs of their lives
to see what I imagine: two images
left on the riverbank, two figures of clay
with rough, thumbed-on faces,
and not gleaming, not holy
but dark with the absence of pity,
an absolute love without knowledge.

I have guessed for my father an innocence
pale as water. He moves through it,
away from me to stride in his sleep
the deep land empty of animals, empty
except for the quick coil of memory
under the foot of his life:
the sure, small dream that kills,
that keeps.

LOUISIANA LINE

The wooden scent of wagons,
the sweat of animals—these places
keep everything—breath of the cotton gin,
black damp floors of the icehouse.

Shadows the color of a mirror's back
break across faces. The luck
is always bad. This light is brittle,
old pale hair kept in a letter.
The wheeze of porch swings and lopped gates
seeps from new mortar.

Wind from an ax that struck wood
a hundred years ago
lifts the thin flags of the town.

AFTER MAKING LOVE

*from the custom among certain American Indian
tribes of returning the bones of eaten fish to the
river from which they were taken*

From pursuit we are bent
toward sacrifice:
fishing these rivers,
one takes on debts.

In the moment of leaping, we remember.
The deep dream will rise
in the moving smoke of our fires.

Now is a handful of bones,
kept whole in the shape of each life,
given back to singular waters.

It is barely enough, this
white song for afterward:
we ask the careful and intricate
blessing
last.

POEM FROM NOVEMBER

The leaves have fallen, releasing the distances.
This year of my turning moves
in an arc like a preying bird's,
purposeful.

My loves have dried. I find
I can remember only the least things:
mouse-gray of my grandmother's hair
dead in the silverbacked brush,
the smell of hardpacked dirt
under black grease in the smokehouse.

Here is the old sky, the one we always had.
Everything in it is small,
punctuation for a vanished story.

I have forgotten the trick
an old man taught me: how the voice
can be made to nest in the cupped hands,
calling. Was it the dove
or the owl I brought close then?
There was a calling.
Something came.

from Nettles (1983)

TOPSAIL ISLAND

January absolves the village.
Summer left no flags. I'm living
just now alone in a room on stilts.
Whatever silts this way is what I've got.

It's clean. Even the fake flowers
left behind on a porch step
are stripped of pretension.
They bloom no-color, original plastic.

Perhaps I am here to practice.

Surely at night these houses break
and sail on perfect silence into the world's
dreams of vacant houses. Then we all move in,
without even a lamp or a suitcase,
until the morning's drydock light
establishes them again, crooked and empty
on their bad knees.

Miles under a blue sun, sand
in my shoes, my heavy parka on:
this is the way the child whispered
I'm the only one.
So many swimmers pulled away from my hands.
Not one of them reached back.
I'm learning the stroke, stroke,
afloat and purposeful along these paths
following a windful of gulls and grackles.

For now, the island's mine, talking
a cold tongue blue,
the light shot through with birds.
The stretch of script behind the tide
I've got by heart,

though every day a new translation
lies down in the clarity of salt.

The shells are millions of new doors, all open.
In the dunes where long grass bends to trace
every tick and tock of wind, the dead
dry fast. Beak and crabclaw hold
what can be held. The tern's dropped flightfeather
knows its own weight at last. Like this
I mean to weather.

TWO WORDS

for Gerald Barrax

Far west of this late afternoon,
mountains I've never seen search California's
sky for snowdrifts. I can only guess
at shapes of trees and flowers
born of such high thrift.
On the flats below, nothing greens.
Rainshadow.
              It is a word for thirst.

In my country, small birds are surging
into October. They gather at dusk,
their pillar of smoke swirling
over the dead chimney,
a dream getting ready to dive,
the fire going backward.
Swifts.
              It is a word for visible wind.

Imagine the lives of such words.
Subtle as the interiors of antique jars,
they shape their enclosed dark
because we hold them to be;
and name after name, they give us the many.

If we should break the clay,
as we can, able to do anything,
believing as we do in no vessel,
believing in fragments, in nothing—
night would step out, the old
wild messenger
bearing the same steep shade,
the same configurations of black wings.

Whatever we hoped to say,
it was there all the time.

THE SWAN STORY

to Don

> *But the youngest was left with a swan's wing instead of*
> *an arm, for one sleeve was wanting to the shirt of mail.*
> —Hans Christian Andersen, "The Wild Swans"

1

If you take my hand
and what you hold is instead
the prickle and broken
knuckles of feathers, dismantled
fingers of flight,
                    stay with me anyway
where we walk in the year's last snow.
If I tell you only a child's tale,
its fragment of singing, its unkempt
puzzle not worth it,
                    stay.

2

Once, wisteria grew round
like a cave or a purple room
where I hid to read long afternoons
that tilted the house and barn toward miracle.

Something flew out of the stories,
my eleven years not yet memory
flapping voiceless and spellstruck
over the derelict kingdom, over
the listing farm, pickets and wild grass,
the exiled orchard.
Without brother or sister, I wore
all the faces, played sibling

to henyard flocks,
pouring out a teacupful of sand.
In graceless tumble and shit-bloom,
possum-robbed, sad-tailed, the hens
scratched their dotty alphabet in dust.

3

In the orchard pond, sun looked
at itself through green.
Frogs leaped into flowers
of shattered light.
The dead mother was a black mirror
where my face wouldn't grow,
its other side only pond-silver,
only the known true world
but hidden still, and unwilling.

Night after night,
over sleep's waters burning blue
in their permanent glacial sun,
I flew the changeable journey,
a cradle of feathers under me,
a kinship, a wonder.
Down there, the day-shadows drifted
undone in the sea's glass dance.
Beautiful as fishes, the nightmares to come
were clotting into reefs.

In dream's icy candescence,
the heart knows how to fall
—*that to fall into darkness*
is to be human awhile—
its landmark the rock-shape of loss.

4

String and tatter, a life
is what it can find

growing wild in woods and churchyard,
houseyard, abandoned orchard.
At the edges where Word *and* Doorsill *die,*
the fieldmouse will stay, and the thrush
under the hawk's eye. The ant will build
at the foot of the apple, and that tree
let down its poor bundles for birds.
There burns the green to be crushed,
to be spun in earth's turn,
the garment our bones wear
weaving itself of humus,
of light the dead are.

Becoming the stung palms of grief.

5

Possums my father blasted from night's tree
lay flat and stiff on the spread mornings,
flies in their teeth;
and the farm's dog nursed a wormhole deep
as an eye socket in the breathing flank,
crossed with bloodless tendon-strings.

How did my mother go
out spark by spark? I could just
remember the box of churchlight,
the strange crowded roses.
I thought she'd left to be
that dun stone angel whose hands were broken off
before I was born into the name it wore.
The whole farm was buried
under a grainy light, the necessary
word sinking deeper with the missing
hands of the stone.

The pantry's vegetable years
dimmed in their jars;

the milk pan glowed like a downed moon
and the wine darkened,
hissing its way up.
On the dark parlor table, a blown-glass swan
lifted clear wings, a flight of rain.

6

Mornings after storms I watched the light
tip its arrows in every brier and bush,
even the possum with his bloody smile,
even the dog eaten down to the bone
and the gravestone clear across town
shining.

Nettle, thorn and sandspur,
the world stings itself into summer.
It can open the hands like stars.

Already the future was threading
green fires. I would startle forward
like the hens shoved out of silence
by the predator's pink bright eye.

7

From love to death to love,
spirit in a splintering bone-cart
jounces, rags and tangled hair,
in silence
always toward the last fire;
and still with its green-burnt hands
weaves.

When the bird—for rescue—alights
like flurries of white air, like snow,
when the body's yet-wanting green
is flung over that whirling flight,

Oh makeshift forever—
dry sticks piled for a killing flame
will burst, every time, into blossom.

8

Broken then
from the heat-blister of childhood
into fragrance of snowrose and firerose,
bud and thorn-nub stirring in flesh
ready to crave and go out,
I woke to no kin but myself
of the long making.
All the winged brothers were folded
under my own skin,
this unfinished shift all I'd have on my back
for the rest of my left-handed life;
all I'd have in one hand this
web, quill and featherbone
to shadow my path with a draggled trace
like a one-sided angel in snow.

Then was the dog unstrung, gone up
like a kite, the worm
blown out of its tunnel.
The hens rose straight out of their tracks.
Tooth by tooth, the possum let go of his grin.
And the stone took up her hands of earth.

9

Long ago the sky came down,
pond water full of refracted birds,
and the grounded kingdom lifted its heavy wings.
In the dark mirror whose face I know,
my mother's hands become a stand of simple weeds.

10

If this is a story, it ends here,
halfway to knowing how.

Only the earliest dream is hollow
and sings. Only that reed
is not filled. Wise bone, flute,
it breathes old stories
into the savage wind that never closes.

Love, tonight we walk in snow
where the creek is nettled with ice.
It grumbles and clinks
beneath a slick suburban moon.
Under flurries that break like pigeons from the pines,
we are freezing and following
rabbit tracks in the blue shadows.
We will laugh our way home, our bodies ready
to clothe each other with hands.

11

What are you and I
but one dreamed story
that out of time breaks into many?
We walk toward our winter fire
under the sky's downfall,
Bird-Loose-Feather whitening our hair.
Dear one, hold on. We are
only halfway there.

FRONT PORCH

for Del Marie Rogers

This is deep-roofed shelter
for a roomful of weather,
the first and last of the journey,

and a boundary you can stand on
from inside or outside
without taking a position.

Anything can meet anything
where household touches wider
world in mud-tracks on the floor.

Here, rocking chairs turn back
on what is left of winter,
bent mourners against the housewall.

We've mostly given it up for lost,
made do with a backyard deck at most.
The cost of that is in direction.

But even now, sometimes, you'll hear one
called home,
that sound like nothing but wind

plucking a long wooden swing
whose arms are full of leaves and lamplight,
shadow-trees on the tall steps, climbing.

REDLANDS

What could going back there claim for me
under the generations of trees,
among shadows thrown like dishwater
from the porches that are left?
Rags of red dust spin in those backroads
like the small storms of Sunday children
raised by nothing but wind.

That girl with dark copper hair, her eyes,
even her skin so nearly the color of pennies
I secretly guessed her Indian—she stood
stiller than anyone in the schoolyard's
redbrick sun. Her presence among the stories,
the ones we never told,
is perfect the way one weathered board is
remembered without reason,
a play of surfaces so ordinary
it can only stay.

Like the Latin that stuck to the roof of my mouth,
the double names of tough farm boys are lost,
those torn out by fistfuls from the ground,
rolling and fighting, stained with red, furious clay.
Without shoes,
they taught us to look away.

How far toward them can I see
this way, one letter at a time?
One leaf after another, October
builds a burning tree.
Both a time and a language, this
gathers at my sleeve and skirt hem,
weather, something about to happen

then. As if I walk there now.
As if I have become that wanderer

who walked on time each autumn into town
carrying a sack, pulling a grindstone.
He went through us, nowhere to nowhere,
by the bad backyards of the year,
his feet raising companions of red dust,
the whole town watching his curse.
Household by household, edge by edge,
he put the shining on.

To shamble out of town then, late,
down the old Attoyac road with its moon high.
To damn the sack of pullets, satisfied
with the few coins, the backsteps faces, and the whine
all day of *dull* against the stone,
its sound like red stars.
The turning sings and sings. That's what there is.

You try to shake that clayey dust. It won't
shake. You'll be back.
Nothing wears out.
You'll light old knives and scissors from the dark.

TO SYLVIA, GROWN DAUGHTER

You who loved so much the creek mud
and the green-shaded woods, all many-
legged moving things, all small hiding
flowers—so like yourself then—
now you are this tall someone
and bright as a fire. Dear lantern!
But listen:

lit with fallen apples and plain grass,
with salamander and birdfeather,
with candles of spring pine,
the old rooms will have waited
the way a forgotten house waits at the edge
of a snapshot you hardly meant to take.
The place has its own moon
and no noise but the cricket's skinny one.

You may enter by the door of what is not yet,
as you did before. Or by the new door
of what has been taken from you.
Pain will let you in, or fury. Ordinary
love will let you in, or any dying.
No key is too odd, no reason too far away.

It is only the house of your first name
that belongs also to the skyful of branches,
to dove, treefrog, and milkweed,
those who begin again.
I say this because it is so simple.
I tell you because it is anyone's.
And because the likeness may be torn
by now, and you may not know.

THE ELIZABETH POEMS

I BOX-CAMERA SNAPSHOT

She stands sharp as a plumb line beside the flowerbeds.
That's July melting the starch in her dress.
Yard dust grits the air, fuzzes the zinnias.

Straw-yellow plaits pulled so tight the eyes slant,
eyes gray as an owl's *who,* she'll wait
among those feral flowers that can grow anywhere.

I can't remember her dream—that ladder
collapsed inside like the skeleton
of some resident starved animal, rib after rib letting go.

She's the one I poke for with sticks,
after the family burials, after the housefires,
in the rubble and smoke of return.

Whose true name couldn't stay, this child's
name nicked and cut back, eked out what is left.
It coats my eyes like ashes or milk.

To see nothing but through this
string figure, lost shoe, puppet broken
out of the play, is less

and more than enough. Out of my hands
the zinnias pop and range, the sun of that year
pumping orange, scarlet, yellow over old ground

nothing should thrive in, the unseen in black and white.
She thrives and wears me like a dress. Her speech
is my sleep, all night the colors of loss discovered.

She will have her desire,
whatever that bone was, even love
counting its missing fingers.

II   Afternoon, Playing on a Bed

Colored sticks leap from her fingers, settle
among marbles cloudy with rose and yellow.
All of an hour she has tossed and made these
be other, out of her hands.
Bumps on the bedspread have marked her thighs.
She rubs how the skin knows
where it's been.
And the grandfather comes through the screendoor streaming
late sun off his shoulders.
Coming a rain. Heard the east thunder.
She knows there can be no weather
until he tells it.

So the red stick she holds is already old
in what she remembers ahead of her: rain is
the wet chickens huddled in their smell of ashes,
brickwalk washed dark and slick, the cistern
pinging. She is stopped barely hearing
the radio hum its *somewhere*
in the Pacific.

No one she knows is in the places
the radio talks. She is here.
And far back in the house, Grandmother
clinks among pots under the kitchen's one-eye.
Lightbulb on a string sways there and throws
her shadow farther than the rope swing goes.
She thinks that shadow
out the back door all the way to the cows.

Yard-weeds lean away from the wet
that is coming. Sun fades in the screendoor,

nightbugs burring where the light has torn.
She wants—
is it to taste this?
Cooling brick, cistern-tin, pink bedspread,
feather, fire poker, rocker varnished with salt:
her tongue knows how each tastes like itself.
Herself, a mouth on her knuckle.

What is so important that it shuts her throat?

Not even the big marble hurting her knee
can make her move. She is spread
over everything like its own taste
and everything is together the way her toes
are on her feet, her arms on her shoulders,
an ache in all of it, this keeping.

Should she cry? The grandfather's listening
to the Pacific, sighing his pipe into sparks.
This, this, she whispers and waits.
It is only summer, only summer and evening.
But might something fumble and miss?
Might the furniture run away like the dog
or the roof crumple down;
might the hens come loose from their hinges
or the grandfather, grandmother   *mother*
come apart like the handful of sticks?
I will hold on tight. But if I can't,
what is the name of what happens?

She is still as she knows to be, the toys
rocking a little with her breath,
and the hard thunder turns over black
and the clacking marbles are falling.
She remembers the name. *Dead*
is the name she remembers. And wakes
to the drum of the rain

breaking its long sticks in the dark
on the round world rolling.

III   Asthma, 1948

Before dawn, the stick-child,
thinned out like a rosebush,
woke crying again. *Hush.*
Accept what the steam kettle offers.
She choked and took in rounds of air.
She gave them back.

Sick days, catalogs kept her quiet.
Hot-colored pages splayed on her bed
bright things that with scissors and paste
could be had.
Nights she dreamed those gold rings
with diamonds like little suns,
her tenth year's skinny finger pointing
        this one   that one.

And she floated like a stoppered bottle
on yellow rings of steam from the kettle,
her message, her *no,* rolled tight in the lung-flesh.
She floated and chose one after another
the bright circlets locked up with stones
for fingers and wrists,
for ribcage and neckbone.

IV   Witness

Begin with a morning.
I take this one,
its old light, its thin
dusty windows.

Look into the backyard. A woman
is standing on two ends of a broomstick

laid on the neck of a hen.
Bending, she grips the shit-caked feet,
jerks the creature loose from itself.

Flung past its own watching
yellow eye, the near thing soars, hits ground,
and scrabbles again into its one strange flight.
Crossing and recrossing the path
of the child whose blue eye is caught
forever in the skein of this travel,
the hen flops and gathers, flings out
the length of what's left.
There is neither time nor any place to be
until the child can stop looking and hen-eye
can stop and the sun be still on the eggful
of blood laid against fenceboards.

Gone cloudy as butter, the one eye looking up from dirt
will shut down its mirror, though something yet drifts
between it and the other, the wind still
breathing out white down-flowers.

Who hazards what the child might remember
or what its value, the woman gone indoors,
the rest of it
what ruined touch or dance after dark
to dismember and chill again?

I have watched this more than once
from a windowsill wholly dust,
myself stockstill in noon light,
hearing the dove's note lift
the only way it ever does, far off.
Yellow and deep blue, the flags
of summer's flowers were blooming
close to home like the gift of sight.

V   FISHING

The rub of that summer warmed her sickroom.
Sticks she gathered with her father

flared in the wind, only blown curtains and fever,
but the picnic fire browned the edge of the dream.
Shadows on the ceiling bloomed
green and speared with sun.
They walked again by the creek
where the fish turned around and came back.

This time the fish are part of the water,
moving too fast to be caught,
their bitter silver breaking the nets of light.
Overhead, the summer leaves
clench suddenly and fall.
Her father hands her a stone to hold,
a piece of flint, an arrowhead.
It speaks into her hand:
this time everything is different and you
have forgotten to bring food.

VI   TRAVELING, 1950

for William Stafford

It is winter. We can just glimpse the moon
passing where the trees are gone.
It is miles of farms, my father driving.
In the heater's flannel air, I'm almost dreaming
black cornspikes and fences. It is then

we pass a house so near the road
we're touched with small, sudden light
from the windows, bolts of dim yellow
flung like silk across a broken porch,
a well in the swept narrow yard.

And caught, the blue-checked tablecorner, chairback,
head-and-shoulders shadow in the frame
that will repeat itself for life, still
the only windows lit for—how far

have we gone? I look
until the distance snaps it off.

My hand pressed to icy glass, I feel
how pure necessity can rise
out there like wind, the moon-grayed land become
different under that wind, a story
always to begin.

Some things are so simple they are seen
exactly true just once, and then forever
the pieces in the mind come back
not fitting anywhere,

clear only then
in poor houselight that clouds our car
as if we are the mirror passed
across a face for evidence,
across a sleeping country where some war
has just commenced.

I say it's nothing. I don't speak of it.
My breath on the dark glass leaves a dripping print.

MINERAL

to my mother, 1902–1944

After the nightmare has flown
its white pennant, after the guesswork
is washed from the life of the lost,
still comes a plumbeous shining
I know as yours, dusklike,
winter on a forest floor.
I keep a piece of porous rock
gives off that smell, the furious
permanence you became.

Thirty-five years late, a grief
the child could not have known to know
is yet nothing like grieving, is only
the long diffuse memory of self
staking out first knowledge of absence.
It is the closest I can come
to mourning's reversible gift.

And clearer than any recall, far
clearer than photographs that have curled
around their faces like babies asleep,
is this featureless strength, stone
lit from within and gathering
rootless shadows close as kin
the way lanternlight does,
making its way in the moonless hour
from houses of the oldest poor.

ROLLER RINK

That summer it just appeared,
like a huge canvas butterfly
pinned to McNaughton's field.
All of us half-grown came every day
to watch and try, in love
with unlikely motion, with ourselves
and the obscure brother
who was older and came from a nameless far end
of the county. He knew, from somewhere,
how to do it, the dance of it turning
faster than music, could bend
and glide smooth as a fish where we fell,
could leap, land and roll on
squatting, backward, one-footed.
We loved him for looking blade-boned and frail,
for being always alone with nothing to tell.

In August the old man who'd taken our change
hefted sections of floor and his tent
and his music into a truckbed and left.
The autumn that came after
rose for us with so perfectly clear
a cry of wild geese and amber light
on its early winds, with so many stars
let loose, and leaves in the rain—
even our shambling, hopeless town
seemed good, just in that turn
before the wheel of the year came down.

Of course it never came again.
There was the round brown place
where grass wouldn't grow in that field,
but would grow next year with great ghost wheels
of Queen Anne's lace.
That summer was a line we'd stumbled over,

and so we were free to fall and gather
the dear, unskillful, amazing losses
departure needs. We took them all,
our bodies shooting crazily
into and through each other. And finally past
to army, city, anyplace far.
We took any road out we could take;
but none of us with the sweet-lifting grace
and ease of the promise that farm boy made
who went and stayed.

THE FARM

Perhaps it comes at night
bearing its own candle.
Or it may come otherwise, to unlight
our daytime task of belief
in the hands' occupations, machines
and their signals, faces of strangers,
the future that repeats in a metal tray.

It comes the way the earthworm's path
becomes part of the traveling creature,
the way creeks wear down rockbed,
and leaves take up
the empty spaces of April.

Have you seen the shape of young corn at sunset,
a gatepost wound with trumpetvine,
the shovel cast down
near a yardful of hens tocking in last shine
of dusk? There is a step of stone
beside the porch, gourds piled beside it,
those uses gone except for color.

How use for color
the aching back, ashes
of drought-murdered bread,
the grip torn free of an iced-over pump?
These too are part of the fields' speech:
the woman irretrievably mortgaged,
the child weakening, the calf dead,
and the man axing wood who sees
his leg suddenly nothing but blood.

Insubstantial as the whuffing ghosts
that drift above the nostrils of cattle in cold,
it rises from our sleep, a smell like sweat.

No more able to lose this than to lose
mother or father, we disguise it
as everything: freedom, guilt,
ignorance, beauty, oppression,
death, innocence. History.

Melons in my grandfather's field
had always one paler side
from touching earth, remembering that dark
with a little loss.
Melon-shaped, the day moons float,
wafers of fever,
over the feeding cities, the dredged rivers.

A televised scientist can tell us now
that crops will someday grow as far
as stations can be nailed to orbit.
As if enameled artifacts in launchpad wires
will sing some song we know; as if
an armored speculum will yet reflect
only time's old furrow and that rain.

As if the dream sent into flight
could take the nightmare with it.
Losing the singular gift, a little risk
to be born into, against,
we shape a world that will become all risk,
as warfare will become all light.

Until, from necessary dark, we take
the real, pared moon we've earned.
Then, knowing what we ask,
we'll ask the ground again
to dream us if it can.
For now, we flinch and drowse.

We plant geraniums in a trench around the house.

REPETITION

Lidded three-quarter
moon climbing live oak's ladder
doubles her face in the owl's mirror.
She is she who called our fathers
waiting by rivershine and twigfire,
wild to gather from wild air
all the fox's dark red feathers.
But fox narrowed and answered never
the old-hearted question in the hunter,
though moonlight spread like blood on water
and the rough crucifix of geese passed over.

Escaped and alone, fox rides the wind's hair,
twists brushfire through the year's weather.
By any river, those footprints flower.
Now *this* moon sings in the tree's fingers,
red-pelted, earth-held flyer.

What hound's cry rides our dark like a mane of fever?

TO MY FATHER, KILLED IN A HUNTING ACCIDENT

R. L. S., 1904–1974

You'd have been waiting all morning
under the flares of longleaf pine
alone with the gun in your arms.
And watching, as you were always watching.
This was the way trees are
under the sun plain as a hand,
such waiting its own place, without time,
and printed with the squirrel's passage
and the small yellow sounds of grass.
The sky of it was the oldest circle
of hawk and sparrow.

Holding the gun, remembering to think
of holding the gun, you held
a lifetime bent to the minor gods
of a particular and passing kingdom.
Its history waited with you—this light
only daybreak on the first kill you shouldered,
this sun splayed on your great-grandfather's bear.
Did your daydream search those red seasons,
knowing each of their beasts,
fur, hoof and jawbone, for a trophy
you could perfectly own?
Did you think again of that emblem, the knife
you once lost by the muddy Sabine, water rising,
you fourteen and lost too on your pony?
Telling that story, you were always sure
the one blade you needed was back there.

I cannot guess your careless thought,
how it unfolded in pine scent,
some strand of memory or need unwinding

too taut and suddenly
broken just *there* on a buried edge,
your father's father's gun taking on
a weight that shifted utterly
                              because of a low branch
rock underfoot or a root
                           the stumble because the world does
turn over   turn over and kill because
the world does and the sound of it
dies out and dies out
in the hot thick light, and ground
can shake like the hide
of a thing enormously alive.

You got to your feet for hours
holding your opened belly,
cicada-hum braiding through red
pain   hope   love   terror
gripping the backbone.

You were standing when strangers found you.

I who am daughter and stranger
find you in every weather of sleep,
the fox's lent eyes seeing for you,
the will of the gutshot deer holding on
where the bobcat in darkness brings out
its wreath of claws, and the smoldering
remnant wolf lays a tribal ghost.

I have nothing to give you but this
guesswork and care; oh careful
as the long women who bring wildflowers
to graves in that country, I place
live birds in the hours you stood for.
And to me you have given a history
bearing up its own animal, the alien
close kin and enemy

who eats in my house
now that the weapons are given away.

Poised in any prayer I make for light,
to catch the way it glances off the world,
your ignorant knife is
praising the river, praising
currents of canebrake, pinewoods,
thickets under the wild sky—
whatever lives there lost,
and whatever is helped to die.

THE CLOUDED LEOPARDS OF CAMBODIA AND VIET NAM

They are gone, almost, into the music of their name.
The few that are left
wait high and hesitant as mist
in the tallest trees where dawn breaks first.

Their color of mourning kindles
to patterns of stark white, random
and sudden as hope or a daydream.
Moving, they could be mirrors of the sky,
that play of masks
behind which the ancient burning continues
to dwindle and flee.

Thousands of years in their bones
leap blameless as lightning toward us.
To come close to what they know
would feel like thunder and its silent afterword.
We would turn slowly on our shadows, look up
again to name the shapes of the world:
monkey, temple, rat, rice bowl, god,
images echoed in the smoke of village cookfires,
in the drift of memory on the faces of elders.
We would stand in the clean footprints of animals,
holding like an offering our hope
for the lives of a handful of people,
for rain that is only rain.

SOUTH WOODS IN OCTOBER, WITH THE SPIDERS OF MEMORY

There's no touch like this one
except (if you remember it) your baptism,
that silent passage through breaking
unbreathable circles of light
where you were caught quaking and brief
in the fingers of clarity.

The world's strung with embraces.

And this air is pearled with a music
far from us but earth-struck
and deep as that water
from which you could wake and wake.

You can never quite see what makes it
to echo and thrum with the taken.

There's just this touch that is not
like a lover's, is more
barely moth-dust and sun-slant,
your eyes new-lashed with it.
You go forward by shudder and wreckage,
bearer of imperceptible message,
brushing the dead from your face.

BLIND SINGER

Her movement's hesitant, close-in, but sure
as if she knew this place but knew it elsewhere.
She never wears, outreaching and unreasonable,
the trust of the always blind. She can remember
what blue distance is and how the shapes of things
are put with light between like membrane.

She plays the local taverns. Her voice
has range and an odd disorder
not quite blues, not quite another thing.
That uncertain edge brings people in,
though she's not graceful under the applause
she knows as a coursing of little stones downhill
or her carpenter grandfather's
bright handful of dropped nails.

And this is most hers: she can't be surprised.
Informed, as madness is, by memory's wild eyes
at windows where only darkness burns,
she sees by turns the world's extremes:
a horse may be a violet, or eggs turn knives,
a dress become a flag, a flag a fire—
the way sleep's rainy mirror lets our lives
become what else they really are.

Still, it isn't dreaming but another
pure combination of consciousness and death,
knowledge without a place to catch, the reel
spinning on and on in the mind's grasp,
the line inexhaustible.

Singing's what she does. And afterward,
in a room with a lit, unnecessary lamp,
she turns a pack of shiny, colored cards.
She turns them all. She turns them all face up.

from Beholdings (1988)

In deep East Texas, we croon to each other. We sing to each other in a high lifted tone, especially in times of greeting or farewell. . . . An East Texan may touch you while talking, just a light touch on the arm or shoulder. The touch is to be sure you don't go away. He is telling you a story. East Texas talks in stories. You have to stay there until the story's done.

—from a column by Gordon Baxter, *San Augustine Rambler*

CLEARING OUT, 1974

After this kind of death, sudden and violent,
there's difference forever in the light.
Here's the sun I'll see from now on,
aslant and keeping nothing
in its backward look. I have become rich
with disappearance. I have become this light

pooled now on my father's desk,
his grandfather's—rolltop sturdy as a boat
and ice-locked in a century of deepening afternoon.
I have to open it and take the cargo on
myself. There's no one else.

Forget the pigeonholes with their indifferently kept
papers waiting to fly out and be important.
They were never important, the cash and receipts,
leases, royalties, mortgages wadded here like trash.
Forget the checkbook that was awash with blood,
and the wallet, its pictures crusted dark.
Everything in his pockets was afloat.
A man shot in the stomach drowns
what's on him. Let the *personal effects*
stay in their labeled plastic sack. Go on

as if this were a forest with a path.
It's like him to have kept a jay's flightfeather,
old now to crumbling, though it holds to blue
like a blind man's memory of sky;
and a terrapin shell bleached of all camouflage,
white dome of cyclopean masonry in scale,
packed with the shape of silence as a bell;
a wild boar's intact lower jaw, the yellowed tusks
like twists of evil weather caught in sculpture,
dusty in a scatter of red cartouches,
the shotgun cartridges gone soft as cloth.

One drawer's half filled with pocketknives,
all sizes, jumble of dark hafts like a cache
of dried fish. Opened, these could still
swim through to sapling heart. To bone.
He had a good eye. With any kind of blade
he'd make a creature walk straight out of wood
into your hand. The few he didn't give away
are gathered here, votive and reliquary:

bear with her hitch-legged cub,
dove in a tree, wild turkey open-winged,
two deer with antlers slightly off
—imperfect the way antlers really are—
and a razorback, a bobcat in a leap.
And then the horses.
My mother gave him real woodcarver's knives,
cherished in their box and not once used.

The best of the figures is the bucking horse,
body like a hauled-back bow.
Even on this scale the strain, the shine
of muscle showing, wind in a flung stirrup.
And all the intricate heave of wished-for power
is drawn down to a block two inches square,
four hooves and the head locked on the moment
arching off that little ground.

Drawerful of keys, marbles, arrowheads, rocks
he saw some form in. Keys to nothing standing.
There's a grace to the thin-shanked instruments
whose ends look like dull claws, the kind old houses
had for every room; blunter keys for barn lots,
cabins that held the violated lives of slaves,
cotton houses, lawyers' offices, stores
that ran on barter.

A peace comes to this sorting.
When my grandmother was a girl, she raised a fawn.

It went wild afterward in our woods. Later,
a buck full-grown thumped up the steps one night
onto the porch outside this very window,
slipping and knocking antlers on the rail.
Framed in the lamplight for one still moment,
the strange known eyes looked in
and the young woman looked out at him.
It's the part of every story we remember,
the dream lost track of, changed
and coming back.

Distance has webbed my eyes like cataract,
thickening like an ice sheet I must lift.
Heavy with damp,
here is the Teal Bible, 1815,
brought to Texas with the first encampment
of Anglo settlers. It's pure living mystery
why they came. Unless mystery's what they came for
after all, with no way to answer it
except the ways to kill; and no new dream enough
to staunch the stubborn longing to recover
what vanished in their footprints.

My great-grandfather's whistle carved of horn.

A cedar knot, deep turn in the red heart
heavy and separate. Nick it, and the scent
of cedar pours out like a sound, that thick.

Wild turkey caller whittled out of pine,
all confirmation gone.

The hunter's horn with one note for the lost.

And a perfect doll-sized real cane-bottomed
chair in a bottle.

That's the lot. I'll take what matters,
blood and documents, to the life I made elsewhere,

that place so far different in this light
you could get the bends between here and there.
The animals in wood, the stones, the silence caught
in terrapin's shell and turkey's pine voicebox,
this desk itself—a beholding full
of time before the tree was cut to build it—
I set all adrift, dismantled vessel, log raft,
rough-layered rings of association
like a language widening.
And the loosed river takes it
toward the turning sawblades of our dawn.

A Greek poet said it. Thémelis:
What would death have been without us?

AYS

I

       The name softens in the bayou,
borne on that murmur, and anchors in wrong letters
on the black bridge marker: the local mispronunciation
            Ayish—anyhow
          it goes on being gone.

       And it must have sounded, said right,
like a cry, like something between a cry and ashes,
         what wind and earth will take.
         So little
           is known of the people who spoke
themselves in it, the spell of their living,
          I think my father—
I think my father with his boyhood's hoard
of scrapers, handaxes, bowls, and arrowheads,
must have held the heavy unhearable echo
         of all that was left to know.

       From the fields at the broken foot
of our farm, from the stony rise that's still
         called Mission Hill,
        he fished their village up,
hearthsites and graves blindsided lightward
        by the shovel-load and scrabble
of a boy's dream-ridden hands in 1915, imagining,
given to imagine, another kind of Indian—
         plains-eyed, horseback and dangerous.

       And when the ceremonial stones
in their perfect pairs, and the points of every size,
the pipes and awls and quick-fired shards,
         were stolen in turn from him,
         in his seventieth year taken

by persons unknown, persons unknowing, who must have sold
the lot to a back-street dealer in Dallas or Houston
        where there'd be no questions about origin,

        then I think my father crying
as one might cry for kin, and not for the simple
serious forms but for unknown echoes around them,
        something never unearthed of his own,
a firesite blackened and fine-sifted as sorrow is
when it cannot be spoken, having become the ground,
        and the longing forgotten:

those magical far-eyed horses that never came.

II

From 1721 until 1773 the Zacatecan Franciscans
passed out bribes and God and smallpox
from one of Spain's more outlandish missions:
Nuestra Señora de los Delores de los Ays.
Abandoned after fifty years without a convert—
in all that time, not one—it goes on sinking
underneath that little hill beside the cow pasture.

In 1807, the Ays were said to be *extinct*
as a nation, there being only twenty-five souls.
No other Indian Nation speaks their language,
though they speak Caddo when among those tribes,
with whom they are in amity. So wrote Sibley,
an agent under Thomas Jefferson.
Today I traded a shawl to an Ays woman
in return for an alphabet. This is lost.

The eighteenth-century travelers' reports
and the few letters from the mission's priests
to the Viceroy (if we set aside the rancor
and the elaborate righteousness) present
a ragtag woodland people with a sense of humor.
Hedonists, by all accounts not violent,

they were fond of the friars' gifts of bluest cloth
because that color was the sky's,
possessed of *the richest lands in all this province,*
given to ease, trickery, festival *mitotes.*
And surprisingly given to hard argument
with any priest who spoke to them of the new God.
An exception is set forth in one report
by a padre who'd told an unintended truth
when he announced to the unconverted
that the God he preached sent pestilence.
For once, he was not disputed.

They were thought to be a fallen remnant
of a people older than the Caddo in this region:
the usual pattern, a disconnected language,
isolation, the dominant tribes' long-held opinion
that these Ays were inferior and degenerate.
Theirs is a story with not much in the way
of imagination, being only a kind of tuneless song
no one has heard, or wanted to.
It was a boreal wisp in the air above our town
and in my father's room where dust had hold
of rows of dim glass cases filled with the dislodged
handwork of the dead, that breakage
drifting always under ours.

Trying to put it together, I come upon
not much more than their small name
the sources spell a dozen ways
so there's no telling it. I come upon
the one kernel of perfect refusal,
and the fever of their whole vanishing
hardens into this:

that they missed the sorry reservations,
the circus of broken treaties, Wild West
shows, dime novels, movies; missed
the scrutiny of ethnologists and moved past

the skewed, befeathered myths we would set up
anew each decade like stuffed birds.
They missed by a whole century the ruinous fervor
touched with Christian resurrection lore:
Ghost Dance rolling down from the Great Plains
to all the fenced and dying-piecemeal cultures,
raising even the docile, changed Caddo,
who'd been removed by then to Oklahoma,
to last-ditch dervishing that failed and failed.

And they are not anywhere for our final turn,
this dance we've always done in our strange will,
our love's distorting lens on what we kill.

This is a story without heroes,
its axis one exquisite fishhook of carved stone,
bone-colored, still sharp, exacting. Taken.

III

I turn from memory and books, translations,
   to speak to the boy my father
where he sits in a slice of the sun of 1915
laying out arrowheads with the dirt still on them,
   wrongheaded patterns on a Turkey rug,

   in the shape-shifting intensity of dream
that would burn for him in the forms behind glass,
be scattered at last like an alphabet unstrung,
   be nameless as ashes or money.

  My father, only this much is certain:
   it was the custom among them
to weep as a greeting to strangers. It was their custom
   to stain themselves red with the clay of this bayou.
They were known by the tribes to be less than the others,
   lazy, not dependable, not brave people.

  They were known to have the best sorcerers.

BIG THICKET SETTLER, 1840s

Aus Hooks watched one ox list like a drunk deacon
and fall stone dead, no reason given
among hummocks and baygalls, ferns tall as the wagon,
oaks and cypresses standing higher than steeples.

Coming into the bottoms, he'd seen a world
unbraked, changeable as the roil of delirium.
Nights were swampfire, nets of mosquitoes
that never let him loose. Dawns like dough.
Rags of fog now tattering past, and the wagon
steep with household suddenly tilting
one-sided as history
with only the one beast to pull it.

Aus Hooks standing and looking:
chair-leg and kettle, harness and mattock
paled in the faint rust-red of wetted dust,
the wagon dampening as if a box could sweat,
trunk and plow handle fading, eaten
like meat in this light, this light

alive with the rivers in it, tides of birds
and an arkspill of animals ungatherable
in gnarling leaflight too clotted
to aim through for a shot. All, all a drowning
downfall rot of trees, vines not even God
could have wanted. Aus Hooks dropped the reins,
dropped *homestead* and *new land,* dropped
under onrushing morning like a worn-out
swimmer under white water,
losing, it might be, even his name
and striking a shoulder hard on the wagon
to remind his flesh of its separate home.

Journey unspooled itself, turning
like the movements of bad sleep on him

in this air that was not rain but smoke
from a green heat burnless. He chose
what his wife would have chosen,
Bible and tintype, and what he'd need.
Then he shot the other ox where it stood,
and he set, among the trunk's clothes, fire
to say whatever it would to the molten
unhaltable kingdom before him, some notion
of *harvest* adrift in his mind like a tune,
while the wagon turned tall as a hayrick and golden.

Had it been possible, he would have thought
a prairie, hard, dry land clean-scoured
to absence waiting to be filled
with what his kind could bring, their work,
their legend, their pining women;
a place that would keep inside
its clear horizon lines and leave him his,
wind and empty weather he'd come to understand
in time. But such a land was not quite yet
available to thought.

Aus Hooks walked back to Georgia, straight
as a pillar of salt.

OIL

First Sour Lake, then Saratoga, then Batson
boomed. By 1905, most of the four-legged
wildcats in the Thicket had been scared
at least once by the other kind.
Panthers got tired of having to move their dens.
The smell of sulphur and the tarry air
that had always hovered kind of familiar
over a few bubbling sloughs
was suddenly everywhere as the underneath
cracked open. Sludge, black scum, and spewed-up
saltwater crawled over pastures and ruined the creeks.
Oil riggers flared the gas all night to keep it
from blowing up. That much light
spooked woods-ranging livestock clean off
and drove the wild game out.

Not that it wasn't hard on all those people
come from damn near everywhere to find
that getting rich meant getting godforsaken
miserable in mud that could sink a whole wagon
and bog a ten-ox team up to the shoulders,
maybe for days. It was hell trying
to get machinery in there, and hell living
in a tent on ground that never dried all winter.
Outside one boomtown, somebody built a railroad
straight into deep thicket to the wells.
When the boom died out, those same men
took up the tracks and left with the whole thing.
It was as if some awful steady, enormous beast
had got born, lived regular awhile,
then vanished trackless as a dinosaur.

At Batson—after what would become
the Paraffine Oil Company had paid the sum
of eighty thousand dollars into the held-out apron

of the wife of one old landowner who couldn't count—
the world turned over: canvas hotels, open-air saloons,
whorehouses, the usual things that rise
when the money's under something else.
But there were some who'd lived in these woods so long
they didn't know they didn't own the land,
and they developed a deep-set opinion
against people poking holes in it for any reason.

The only way the riggers could get in
or out of the Thicket was on horseback
single file, and even that was hard.
One time, when a worn-out crew came off the derricks
and headed to where they'd tied the transportation,
they found their horses seriously changed.
Upset nesters had got themselves some paint,
every kind of color they could find.
Maybe the riggers thought a vengeful dream
had come for them out of the awful ground
when they saw those horses shining in the sun,
wet, some of them striped, every way looking wrong.
And worse, damned near too jumpy to ride home.

If you could call Batson exactly home,
tent carnival smeared with the black smell of oil,
riches so new there hadn't been lumber cut
to build anything quite real, the jail
a couple of big trees where prisoners were chained;
and people spilling from Ireland, New York, England,
jumped-ship sailors next to out-of-work cowboys,
speculators, thieves, peddlers, swindlers, killers,
living too close together in a haze of sulphur.

Around all that, the Thicket sweated,
breathing in and breathing out
paraffin mire, thorns, snakes, sweet cash, and a few
stray puzzled deer right onto main street
where even the idea of oil was new, though the stuff

had once been bottled from the seeps
by a half-Indian who went by the name of Doctor Mud
and wore a top hat, claiming miracles.

Now here in a twilight of owls and ivory-bills
came twenty horses passing strange,
bright cayuses of Apocalypse, a string of fevers—
greased, half-crazy, cut-loose carousel
   blue   yellow   orange   barn-red
with mad roustabout riders not able to guess
which way they'd be changed themselves
when the whole shebang pulled out for good,
brass-ring rich, wounded, broke, cured, or dead.

STORIES, 1940s

For example, Oscar Sawyer's store.
Out front the lone gas pump was red,
the kind already long past use,
a skinny sentry with a head of glass.
The store itself listened toward the road,
leaning by inches in the direction of news
without much more forward margin.

I don't have to tell you how old men
sat outside on wooden drink-crates in good weather,
how they watched. A boy might come by with a pup
or a sack of pecans to sell or trade.
You know what was on the shelves inside:
potted meat, sardines and crackers, rusty traps,
glass candy-jar clouded with sugar dust.

A mile or two back of the store,
Indian village and Spanish mission
slept together two centuries under
Jenkins' farm. That far down, the bones
of the Ays and the priests exchanged conversions,
heat-shimmer on green ears of corn.

Hosey Lucas was always there at Oscar's.
He looked like a man made out of parched cornhusks.
People said that. People waited in the lull
when no car was passing. They knew he'd tell
again how he happened to have that sunk-in place
right in the middle of his forehead—
kicked by a mule when he was twelve
and the whole thing just healed over
without a doctor. Left him potholed
deep enough to set a teacup in,
and he still had good sense.

He might tell about the coon that jumped
straight out of a tree onto Garsee Johnson's back
and rode him home.
Or about the time old man Burton found a track
in the dirt road by his house and thought a snake
that didn't ever wiggle must have made it,
so he got his gun and trailed the thing for miles.
Came up on a bicycle rider resting in the shade.
The old man, who'd never seen a town,
stayed mad a week.
Hosey Lucas and his dog would sit.
And both of them could talk.

Behind them, all the corn could do,
it did—telling long bones, dead fires,
arrows to the sun, the deepening ceremonies
in a new translation.

In far-off places, the future's story began again,
SS gun butts breaking children's heads
completely, the small animals of some woods
unable to live, or even to run in the human heart.
At Los Alamos, people started taking things apart.
Fireflies would spark up early at Oscar's.
Somebody'd say fox hunting had got harder,
like you couldn't hear the dogs as good.
And somebody'd come back with, "You just too old
to hear, period."
The dam that in twenty years would take their land
was edging toward a drawing board,
that phantom water
already muting the fox's plume
and muffling the hound's high laughter.

These dirt farmers would die soon
in their beds, or fall down in a barn.
The red dust wouldn't notice that they'd joined.
Not so you could tell it,

though there might be some kind of difference in the form
that dances in dust-devil wind. If we could see it.
People then could still die in one place,
in the illusion of one piece
of time, and take a wholeness with them into earth
the way an apple does, fallen in tall grass,
unnoticed until nothing's left above ground
except the story, *apple,*
bitter or sweet or poisoned as the real,
and ready for reenactment in the round.

Everything was quiet but the bugs
at Oscar's, nobody talking one August afternoon
when the field of black-eyed Susans across the road
took on an extra layer of the light,
a thickening like before a cyclone. And not like that.
Things went dry as a sermon, too still,
as if the air had emptied its glass bottle
just for a minute. Then somebody opened a knife
and peeled a green stick, one long curl
with the sound it makes: a whisper, then a *tick.*
And cleft Hosey Lucas leaned back, mentioning the world.

DIGRESSION ON THE NUCLEAR AGE

In some difficult part of Africa, a termite tribe
builds elaborate tenements that might be called
cathedrals were they for anything so terminal
as Milton's God. Who was it said
the perfect arch will always separate
the civilized from the not? Never mind.
These creatures are quite blind and soft
and hard at labor chemically induced.
Beginning with a dishlike hollow, groups
of workers pile up earthen pellets.
A few such piles will reach a certain height;
fewer still, a just proximity.
That's when direction changes, or a change
directs: the correct two bands of laborers
will make their towers bow toward each other.
Like saved and savior, they will meet in air.
It is unambiguously an arch and it will serve,
among the others rising and the waste,
an arch's purposes. Experts are sure
a specific moment comes when the very structure
triggers the response that will perfect it.

I've got this far and don't know what
termites can be made to mean. Or this poem:
a joke, a play on arrogance, nothing
but language? Untranslated, the world gets on
with dark, flawless constructions rising,
rising even where we think we are. And think
how we must hope convergences will fail this time,
that whatever it is we're working on won't work.

THE KINDS OF SLEEP

First there's the one in which all the children
your parents wanted you to be are chosen.
The sheep from the goats they said in Sunday school.
You remember judgment: it's cool as blue marble,
quiet as a hospital. All the others
have been led to honeyed pastures—
is that it? Anyhow, you are the only goat,
stuck in a stone place with your own sad smell.
Nobody cares if you wake up.

You may sleep to believe in ink.
It seems to be ink but there's more of it,
viscid, a blot that will cover everything.
And with no words in it, nothing but black.
You have been made responsible. So you push,
you push to save whatever you can from the dark.
It seeps through your fingers, gets worse.
For a whole mysterious night you have to be Sisyphus
lacking a stone, wrestling an angel of pitch,
the black in *black plague,* the perfect
coherence of floodwaters.
You give your right arm for an edge.

Then there's the walking sleep.
It's dark, but somehow the right house
assembles itself under your feet.
You step into air and it's there,
the kitchen with the pie-safe and pictures
of white roosters, the dining-room window
framing oak trees and the fishpond;
the rooms with their sentinel fireplaces
coming to be in your footfall.
A thorntree of fear grows in your throat
when you remember the house
will end, used up, at the porch rail

beyond which the rest of your life
is creating you step by step.

Last is the sleep with flowers
and the golden fishes you have come to feed,
a child with raw oatmeal in your pocket,
zinnias in your leftover Easter basket.
This is the sweet one. You have forgotten
everything except morning where it is always morning,
and your ignorance surrounding you with green,
with presence, with your body that can merge,
like the pomegranate on its tree by the fence,
with light. All that you never want to know
has gone, has not come. You slip off the last
porch step into the dewy grass, the path
to the pool where goldfish break black water
that folds again into night above their lanterns.
The goat in the pasture lends you his eye of surprise
as the world fails and you step onto white
    bedsheet   feathers   paper   snow
on which you will lie down, not even flailing
an angel shape, not breathing your small tune, not
writing your name.

REMEMBERING BRUSHING
MY GRANDMOTHER'S HAIR

I see her in a ring of sewing, light
fingers on needle and hoop, elaborate
scissors shaped like a tiny stork,
the glass egg in her lap.
Her temperate mourning wore black shoes.

Released, her hair released a scent
as I imagined of ascending birds, or smoke
from a burning without source, but cool
as mist over a real country, altars in the hills.
That gray reached all the way to the floor.

A cloak, wind in a cloak, her hair
in my hands crackled and flew. I dreamed her
young and flying from some tallest room
before she had to let her power down
for something to take hold and climb.

Permanence. Rose and vine were twisted
hard in silver on the brush and mirror.
Above us, the accurate clock pinged:
always on a time there comes a sleep
stony as a tower, with the wild world beneath,

and wound like this with locked bloom tarnishing—
I brushed, She sewed or dozed. The child I was
stood shoulder-deep in dying, in a dress of falling
silver smoothed by silver, a forgetfulness
dimming the trees outside the window like a rain.

To grow to stay, to braid and bend
from one high window—
I guessed the story I would learn by heart:
how women's hands among sharp instruments
learn sleep, the frieze like metal darkening,
the land sown deep with salt.

RENT HOUSE

I can't think why I've come to see this
house with no resonance, temporary
years between the real houses: that one
I was born to, the other I traveled from.
The interim is here, habitual, stupefied
summers of brass and blue enamel,
smudged backyard grass of fall.
Everything that was here still
stands except the cannas. The journey
of the same cracked two-strip driveway
ends the same.

Before this, the short life it feels like dreaming
to remember: field and barn, pecan trees,
the rambling gentle house holding its own
wide skirts of pasture, fluttering henyard,
and my live mother close.
The town doctor's had that place for thirty years,
all the pecans, sunset behind the fence rail,
a bed of asters in the filled-in fish pool.

The last of childhood left me in yet another
house, five unsteady porches, grandparents,
a spread wing floating me along until I simmered
into leaving.
Years ago, a retired contractor from Houston
restored that one to unremembered splendor.

This narrow house between.
I look a long time, thinking
I need imagination, but there's nothing
to be made of such temporal defeat.
How long was it we lived on this back street
behind screens billowing with rust?
I remember how long one afternoon

I wrote my whole name broad and hard in crayon
on every single windowscreen in this house,
and then was punished.
Forsythia is the name of those flowers
I watched darken in the wallpaper.

All night I'd listen to the child next door
cry and cut teeth. Now he's a lawyer
in San Francisco. I matched his howls
with those I kept back. Both our voices
ran down the moony street alongside crossed
adult allegiances that roamed, like ghostly wolves,
the nights of any town so old.

Nobody rented in a town like this.
Why did Papa bring me here
to this aunt who makes me braid my hair?
Where is my mother?
Where's the calf you said was mine?
What happened to the trees?
Then they'd drive me out there so I'd see
fields dizzy with briers, the derelict house
large and sad and creatureless.
Until I lost even my loss, got used
to a cramped hallway and a makeshift life,
the tight backyard with no hen in it.

And it was here I staked a claim: from any room
I could look up to see my name
purple or lime green against the sun,
or clearer, lamplit on the night outside.
Nothing they tried would get it off
those years I thinned down, toughening,
asthmatic with grief and discovery:
how the self, amazed, swam up like bone
through the lost landscape, through the mother's
vanished flesh, through all remembered
and all future home,
to build garish letters on the riddled air,
knowing there's no place else. Not anywhere.

CORNER OF PAWNEE AND BROADWAY

Canst thou bind the unicorn
with his band in the furrow?
—Job 39:10

Beached on a Wichita street corner
by three-dollar wheat, drought, and the general wind,
he wore the inevitable wide-brimmed hat
hiding his eyes that anyway would tell us
nothing.
       He stood beside a harvest that would sell,
paintings-on-velvet brought from Texas by the gross:
Rambo full-length, deft, akimbo with weapons
against a softened night;
John Wayne close up, squint and jawful of heft.
Last, and lined up straighter than the rest,
sweet-faced unicorns, white as Christmas,
on a dime-store sparkle of planetary dark.

"I used to be a wheat farmer," he said.
"Three-quarters of my sales is unicorns.
I don't know what that means."
We hadn't asked. We left him looking weathered
as driftwood in a phosphorescence
of raised fists, Saturday-cartoon desire
glittering on the spiral horn no creature
but the narwhal ever wore.

Corpse-whale. Sailors in the Middle Ages
thought it augured shipwreck.
And they risked it, bringing back the ornament
merchants would sell by inches to the richest
terrors of the time, and set in gold to dress St. Mark's.
It passed for proof against poison, solar zenith,
virgin lure—and into holiness:

the horn not a horn, the unicorn not
even approximately the hiding real
neutral beast of the neutral sea,
spinning its peaceful courtship emblem
long and long in the meadows of the ice.

The plains wind laps at ruin. Less and less
can stick to the tacky nap of grief
out here where farms fall into dark as if
the Kansas sky had slung
its twisting harpoons everywhere at once.

And all the stories get each other wrong.

CAPE SOUNION

This light is never silent,
washing the rocks with loud blue,
clamoring in wild flowers—
tocsin of blood-red poppies,
sanctus of *peruka* and *narkissos.*
It hides a lyre in the shaken temple
whose marble sings false white
to every boat.
Seen close, the stone is harsh,
hoarding the gold of deserts and their lions
on the long throats of the columns.

Words. Here are the travelers: English,
German, Italian—the dates of our centuries
scratched on the pillars. Byron's name
struck high and silly.
Nothing we've attached dulls the assault
or contains it. Or can make open
any door to leak us whole
through this aurorean rumble.

It's sheer luck, our being here
alone—no picnickers, no tourist buses—
with the old salt god and our inadequate praises,
and the whole day falling clangorous down the sky.
We've pocketed the useless,
music we remember, change, sunglasses.

A broken relief too poor for the museums
leans against a foundation. It shimmers
and thrums in the beaten grass: half a horse,
its one eye gone, mane barely preserving the wind
and the panic. One foreleg is raised terribly
against the drone of loss.

The image has caught us
as if a net went out from it
woven entirely of rift.
If we listen, we will be taken
and partial forever, given half
to rubble and grass, the rest
a bronze note struck with such force
all outline
will be driven back into stone,
defeated form humming under the skin.

If we listen.

Only the merciless light
rides a whole horse on these mountains.

THE CASE FOR GRAVITY

Hydrangeas bloomed beside the house,
globes of blue light blurring in the rain
that finally broke the gold, hot pane of summer
that summer I was five.
I leaned from the high porch-edge over a sea
that spread, sudden as creation's, in the flower bed.
All afternoon beneath the unclenched sky
our tin roof sang small change.

And the drenched oak had dropped a few
mutable leaves. Five-finned they floated,
multiplying as if the wind
meant something new.
I reached with a bent pin on a string,
fishing until I leaned too far and lost
my hold on the house. Time turned then
all space, all bright blue slow drift

of planets sheared entirely loose for one
stopped second when it seemed I flew
or swam in nothing. And the nothing swam.
I flopped hard, like a trout,
on the world gone bust, blue bits of it
floating sweetly down the pewter air
as I stood up baptized with mud,
a pain like bands of bells around my head,
blood in my eyes.

After the first fall, there are the others:
vertigo's possibilities, the love
like a dropped cup, all hope
spilled so out of reach the world lets go
to bluest distance.
                              Always the ground

reels me in to its cruel flowers, nothing ideal,
blue taste of beauty on the bitten tongue.
Say this time too I'll stand
mud-colored, abloom with bruises, vivid with news.

Say these are sheaves of fishes in my hands.

from The Difficult Wheel (1995)

REVENANT

Horizontal in my green coat,
resting my head on a log, I must have seemed
some part of autumn that refused to turn,
under the flicker's scissoring and the squirrel's
scribble against an iron sky.

And this is a simple story. Let loose
it will run by itself to the place
where blanched sun laced through near-bare branches
and the day seemed to pour from the hawk's gyre.

To doze in woods is to rest on the hard edge
of fear, so you're awake
to what you can neither see nor dream
nor come at with a name.
And yet I thought at first of hikers
in that crash of leaves, a sound that dimmed
at the edges then came back all wrong
because there was no order in it,
no human rhythm.

I did not quite cry out but froze the moment
I saw him see me, saw the heavy-antlered head
alter its slant.
He moved in the slow way animals will seem
to move in children's picture books,
on each page larger, clearer—
until he was so close I saw the shine
on raised black nostrils,
and I thought stupidly of creeks,
how they go black with mystery
underneath the winter's lens of ice.

Browsing the leaf-quilted floor, huffing,
the deer edged closer, stopped, his eyes on mine;

and the moment went sly as a dream, the world
unhinged a little, light with reckoning and change.
But there was no revelation. None.
No help for the poet's old protean
longing to become, to be undone.

Whole minutes—two? three? A look, a tangle
of otherness tight as bramble, odd
as a long fall. Nothing
had ever happened or ever would
while I could hear that stranger-breath and see
each separate shoulder-hair shift color as he blew
a snort like a horse's. How exact the hoof's design
on fallen leaves, lifting and setting down
with such small sound I might be still alone.

And someone now is saying this is one of those
dense and symbol-laden moments poets make
to force and tease, the whole thing false
with sexual curvature and hidden weight.
This could be the father coming back
in the form he killed. Or the father's
nemesis. Or it could be a sweet communion,
that old lie.

Finally huge and motionless as a tree
and nearer than my senses wished to know,
he took on, like a cloak, the simple dusk.
And if that looks like poetry, like loss,
the shadow of loss, or memory like black water
on his sides, then let it be
these words as good as any.
                                He leapt straight up
as if to lose that covering thought.
He turned and caught
the barest gilding of last light
and stirred the leaves to sharp explosion
and was gone. A distant brushy rustle.

It took me longer to begin to leave.
Some tears shook from me without regret or reason,
a kind of backward praise. For what,
I neither know nor quite forget.

PROPHECY

with a borrowing from Stevie Smith

The poets have gone out looking for God again,
having no choice,
disguising as typeface, mirror, theory's fretful counterturn
the old search in the voice.

The trees still wave, green as a summer sea.
The grain still makes in the ear
a richness we can almost hear.
And the world still comes to be. And not to be.

Nothing has changed, really, we whisper,
though all we trumpet is the changing stir.
And the air is emptied where they were:
spirits, gods, demons, with whatever

named them gone like fallen wind.
Did we imagine they had wings?
Perhaps they thought they did,
until we learned and flew ourselves, singing.

They went out the way stars do, slowly,
the long centuries of flight
unspiraling from them. They melted quite
like Icarus or those figures of ordinary

murderers and monarchs remade in wax museums.
Like these, they lack all metaphor
to tell what they were for.
And we lack any means to . . . any means.

What we do have is light. See how they are still burning—
all those classical noses, Coyote's laughing muzzle,
Shiva's raised foot, Christ's cheek, the dazzle
of leafy-armed women darkening, ashy-turning.

With this candle to see by, the poets are calling
and calling, much further out than they thought,
not kneeling but falling.

FOUR FROM THE SPIDER

Enact yourself between fixed points,
but loosely—let the wind anoint
clarity with death, and death with light.
Live on the sheerest opposites.

Dance in a thin but working order
Choreograph a net that severs
with just such difficulty as
makes it worth the making-over.

Take what comes, food or the random blown,
with indiscriminate self outspun.
The world is everything that sticks.
Choose. Then count illusion's tricks.

In the season's final filament be caught.
Nothing—not saving grace nor closing argument—
attaches to your having been
the wheel you turned in.

ONE OF A KIND

The mule is offspring of an ass and a mare, combining the strength of the horse with the endurance of the ass. It is incapable of procreation.
   —dictionary definition

Consider the mule, thick as a stump,
clay-flecked and ugly in any of several
dismal colors. His knobbled bones hold up
neither one true kind nor the other.

Made like a conjecture,
he stands in his singular inch
of time, the present tense
he runs in order to perish of it.
Over and over, he dies out.

No wide-flung history of *horse* can race
in his stalled sleep, no wind's long-running story.
The future will foal through him no trace
of the delicate-paced small ass of the sand
or the heavy wild hoof of Mongolia

to say the blood and earth continuous.
I think even the utterly domestic
dray and donkey remember in their dreaming flesh
all that it matters to remember:
America's tall grass wandering unfenced,
Spain chinked with cobbles, Arabia breasting
the desert. And how the little streets of Jerusalem
were lit blue with evening,
winding like veins toward the heart.

Not this one. Born canceled, he works and balks,
angry always in the muscle of his unknowing,
himself his only tribe, and that one going.

He waits in his rubbly coat for dark,
rowing and rowing the stony field,
turning the difficult wheel.

He bears hard goods of this world on his back,
and the black whip and the man who wields the whip—
the man who is angry too, sensing the serious kinship.

VALENTINE AT FIFTY

Too many times I have left you.
I grew isolate as a tide pool, stubborn,
all my broken-into houses scattered.

I missed you then, the inward-turning
curve exposed and shining, the designs
of the sea's voices all over

everything. You were patient in my silences,
though you must have been sad, beachcombing,
looking for whole animals.

This is to say a vow again beside our February sea,
bone gray as any history. *I love you.*
Useless phrase. I carry it like a thing
picked up in the dunes, some crab claw
or ancient tooth, under the shadow
of the careening gull.

Saying it, the mouth still
goes through all its phases,
whole moons opening and closing.
And in it we still hear our own blood's spiraling
sibilance like the shell's, and the horizon's
distance, red and purple siberite now whole,
now touched with paths of breakage toward the dark.

THRESHOLD

They are brittle, tucked carefully as saved letters
into the envelopes of their heavy coats.
You've seen them in the park
they think might be the bad forest
in the storyteller's heart.
Holding up faces pained as newborns',
they seem likewise never to have meant
to reach their destinations.

You've seen how they move, the lame
halting, the halt on the tortuous lam.
Partly it's the body's faulty music
and partly a dodge, a circumvention
of rhythms they no longer want to keep.
This tedious stealth is more than fear
of being mugged, of falling or running out
of breath that laps too shallow at their ribs.

They are slowed by newer wounds: this April
sharpening its countless blades, too green.
Too green the new leaves. Too red the burst
run-over squirrel and the gang of tulips on the hill,
extortionists. See the shawled old women wince
at heated pinks azaleas proffer, at goldfinches
alight, and morning-brightened gutter water.

Even the white hillocks of an old man's own
knuckles in the sun will seem too much.
Things will not dim. No matter how the eye
squints out the day's blue fires,
the dogwood in the wind's a riot
of shooting stars.

And this accounts for cataracts, for deafness
feigned or real, for the narcotic ache

and lost recall, for the retreat
into a sepia past, into the simpler
terror of the prowler and the maniac.
Hope will keep the body and its soul
indoors, content with the equivalents
of hotplates and thin, discolored cats.
Though all the shades drawn down will not
narrow the light one whit, nor stay
the hundred burning tongues of forsythia.
The tighter the bolt, the wider open
our one embrace is flung
from flesh to the wild, marauding garden.

NEW SOUTH

It's lovely where we live. We chose it
maybe because there aren't grapevines or blackberries.
This neighborhood is all those natural-seeming
yards that cost so much to keep them seeming
natural. The city's nice enough. And far enough away.
Sometimes I remember there are no graveyards here,
no stone angels standing on the dead,
ready to take to the air but staying.
Nobody seems to *be* dead. Where are they?
If they were ever here it isn't mentioned.

The friends I've made are smart and talented.
And I know them all so well I might imagine
they are myself. Almost. There's a prickly quick
energy in them, a kind of light. I borrow that.
I borrow. Lately some of them have borrowed back:
they're buying antique quilts to stretch and hang
like paintings on their walls. And something in that
shocks me—scraps of nameless lives hung up,
not warming anything in those white rooms
so like my white rooms. So why should it feel strange?

I have a dozen quilts myself, all marked
with the names and dates of ancestors who made them,
and folded in a chest as old as they are.
How blame my friends for buying what I thought
you had to have already, make, or never have?
Or for hanging quilts like art instead of keeping
use alive? I guess it's part of the whole past
it was so terribly important that we lose.
And then enclose to look at in museums.
Still, I like a horizontal seeing,

looking at history. My quilts stay what you might call
active—it reminds me of the time I volunteered

with the Elder Center out near Holly Springs.
Those country women quilted every Thursday,
and the social worker who runs the place told me:
It's sad. They could sell these quilts so easily
if they didn't use those polyester pieces
and ruin the authenticity. I told her then
that you use for quilts whatever the life has used,
and if that's some of polyester then it's right.

Because isn't that what being authentic is?
I could get mixed up between *preservation*
and *nostalgia* tacky as polyester. I know
the past's not real. And never was, somebody said.
You can hang it up one way (like Williamsburg)
as what you want. Or hang it another way
as what you fear. Either one will change it.
Once I saw Native Australian sand paintings
reduced to manageable size, made permanent
with glue or canvas so we could take them in.

And they were fine to see, but they'd given up
the ritual that lived in their huge temporary form:
the ground itself, even wind that had to scatter
the pattern, all lived as part of the necessity
of making. Lately I've not been quite sure
what ground I'm standing on. As if I'd waked
in Belgium after starting out for Beaumont—
and with this hurtful worry, a kind of sickness
for things changed or missing, things that pass,
the air around me thick and still. Like glass.

VOYAGES

We were five girls prowling alleyways behind the houses,
having skipped math class for any and no reason.
Equipped with too many camelhair coats, too many cashmeres,
we were privileged and sure and dumb, isolated
without knowing it, smug in our small crime, playing
hooky from Miss Hockaday's Boarding School for young ladies.
Looking for anything that wouldn't be boring
as we defined that, we'd gone off exploring the going-downhill
neighborhoods around our tight Victorian schoolgrounds.
The houses were fronted with concrete porches,
venetian blinds drawn tight against the sun.

Somebody had told us an eccentric lived where one
back fence got strangely high and something stuck over
the top. We didn't care what it was, but we went anyway,
giggling with hope for the freakish: bodies stashed and decaying,
a madwoman pulling her hair, maybe a maniac in a cage.
Anything sufficiently awful would have done.

But when we came close enough to look through
the inch of space between two badly placed fenceboards,
we saw only the ordinary, grown grotesque and huge:
somebody was building a sailboat bigger than most city backyards,
bigger almost than the house it belonged to,
mast towering high in a brass-and-blue afternoon.
This was in the middle of Dallas, Texas—
the middle of the 1950s, which had us
(though we didn't yet know this) by the throat.
Here was a backyard entirely full of boat,
out of scale, out of the Bible, maybe out of a movie,
all rescue and ornament. It looked to be something between
a galleon and a Viking ship, larger than we could imagine
in such a space, with sails and riggings and a face on the prow
(about which we made much but which neither smiled nor frowned).

Gasping, overplaying the scene, we guessed at the kind
of old fool who would give a lifetime to building this thing.
Then one of us asked for a light for a cigarette
and we all knew how easy it would be to swipe
a newspaper, light it, and toss it onto the deck
of that great wooden landlocked ark, watch it go up.

But of course we didn't do it and nobody of course came out
of that house and we of course went back
in time for English and to sneak out of P.E. later
for hamburgers at Mitch's, where the blue-collar boys
leaned in their ducktails against the bar.

But before we did that, we stood for a while clumped
and smoking, pushed into silence by palpable obsession
where it sat as if it belonged on parched Dallas grass,
a stunned, unfinished restlessness.

And didn't the ground just then, under our penny-
loafers, give the tiniest heave? Didn't we feel how thin
the grass was, like a coat of light paint, like green ice
over something unmanageable? How thin the sun
became for a minute, the rest of our future dimming
and wavy and vast, even tomorrow's pop quiz and softball practice—

as if all around us were depths we really could drown in.

THE WOMAN HIDDEN IN THIS PAINTING

Like a renegade summer she begins
to burn outside defining lines
almost as if a child's hand traced
and lost her.
Window, leaf, bird, the stony hill
absorb her until the body's only
a put-off dress, a color vanishing
so slowly the watcher in his trance
misses it entirely.

Now a lifting as if her arms are lifting,
a soaring sheer
stretch—and her skin is air.
Or say a string of beads has scattered
and the whole light gathers them
invisible in bright haze
as the pear that might have rested
where morning struck such shine from the table.

One rose-gray feather on the sill
implies the silk-on-silk of dove call
she might hear. Just there,
the open curtain would brush her fingers
and the plain white cup obscure
her wrist unbraceleted.

One line might draw her back, a traveler again
in flesh upon a track of bone,
to cast against the sun-drenched wall
a shadow, dark heel knit to her heel,
time plangent in the bell-bright blue
shawl on her shoulder. See
how she was and will be here,

a dream staining the light the painter
has forgotten?

Beyond, beyond the half-open curtain,
the apron of grass is, and ribboning
paths hemstitched with chicory.
Farther still (Oh the eye is endless)
dark trees feather a restless sky.
She will return in this, a mist
at her throat, her arms reddened
with horizon. The gray of the hare's flank
is the gray her eyes give back.

And pale. The face when we have seen it
will be pale beneath the glow
the wind's pearls told her.
Presence, she whispers,
a changing
chink of weather in the window.

TIME AT THE MOVIES

Say we move through our days some way secure
in other people's moments,
each one of us a star in several reels
of the lives of any number of our friends,
our relatives, our enemies.
We're parts—sometimes walk-ons, sometimes leads—
in separate plays that replay in the minds
of those we know
know us.

That party where the drunk blew up
and you were heroic. Or useless. What you were.
And the awful night that love affair left off,
when you were absurd, or reasonable, or cruel.
And on that toppled birthday, didn't the wrong
present tumble from the box?
Then once, for reasons you've forgotten,
you made your father cry.

Someone remembers. If not as you remember,
at least in the neighborhood,
though circumstance and outcome may be changed,
and the color of your hair and what you said.
Never mind how various and unstrung
the world: it still is *you*
in that mind's eye, flickering.

Imagine all of us together in one place,
each person holding strands that reach to *then*
and you in it: eighth grade, the summer after college,
the year you had that dog that may have been
all black, or white with brown spots.
And you hold lines to all the other pasts,
the people in them.

They in your life and you in theirs are like
a city full of lights one sees by
whether there's a moon or not.
Or like lights crossing underwater, unmistakable
but wavering so you cannot see the source.
And with it all a kind of music, voices
dissonant, disarranged as dream. We move
by what you could call keeping time.
And now and then a tug on some taut line
can bring you up still gasping and still you.

Now imagine, little by little
the skeins of light, the sounds crisscrossing,
start to scatter and to dim
the way a house will darken bit by bit
as one by one the people there turn in
to dreamless sleep, talk fallen into quiet.
But you, stalled wherever you are, stay sure
of conversation and entanglement,
of bright beams trolling the dark,
though the pantomime
goes fast to shadow or to snow.

Until you sense the blank the world's become
and you forget yourself.
And they are gone.

ILLUMINATIONS

I don't know when he died. When we were children,
we thought he must be older than the river.
The flesh on his long bones had gone
from black to gray, as if inside him
some drowned lamp was rising.

Every afternoon he cut the lawns,
sometimes with a scythe, a thing
we had no name for yet.
And no one spoke his name to us.
Everywhere he went he took the crooked
but oddly graceful walking cane he'd made
of burnt-out flashlights soldered end to end
and finished with a piece of tapered wood.

In town he tapped it hard, as if for attention,
for something he might be about to say.
And when he worked the yards, it shone
out of the grass where he'd laid it down
like Aaron's rod or some magician's
silver wand, its bright red buttons
lined up straight, its thumbed shiny switches.

Of course we made up what might happen if
he ever played that instrument,
what might glow or be snapped off,
and whether good or bad would leap
in the power we thought it kept.

And when he'd disappear for weeks or months,
we made up matchless reasons for his going.
We gave him the richest thing we had: our fear
of all real mystery. We had so much to figure out
of what went on around us in the dark,
it was what we knew best: not knowing.

Those last years, he gave up work—even the churchyard—
and took to walking every hot dirt road
in the whole county, and every street around
the courthouse square, his stick still gleaming,
tapping and raising dust.
We'd follow sometimes, at a distance, quiet.

I believe we thought he'd turn to us and tell it,
whatever it was. Or turn on us with it.
Then at least we'd either know, or have to run—
we had a question but we didn't know what question.
Of course he never even turned.
Did we?
        I can't remember when we lost him,
when we forgot
                to look for him in riddles of our own.

It would be years before we'd see the light.

"IN ANOTHER LIFE . . ."

People will say it at parties, speaking of the shock
one feels at being quite familiar with some place one's never been,
or with a face not seen before. Again
last night I heard it from a friend just home
from the south of France. And years ago I knew a man
who'd say it meaning something else entirely. He'd bring
whole strings of former incarnations in to dinner.

But those chronologies are wrong.
The other life exists, if it exists, alongside this one.
If there were maps for such strange latitudes
they'd read: *unchosen parallel.*

In mine, these hands learned calm and gardening,
the catch of fabric against a roughened palm,
the steam of canning kettles, jelly-making.
In the lifeline of that shadow-hand, I stayed.
Say I married a man from the county. He sells insurance
in the town. Really just a farm boy
who lucked into another living
because it was the 1950s and you could.
Still, our garden is the biggest one around.

We have children, grown now and ordinary as potatoes.
They didn't really know how to surprise us.
We had plain troubles, hard but workable.
One son went into business with his dad.
I think I teach at the high school
the way my mother did
before the path approaching me divided.
The old poems make me oddly happy.

And my father spent his age with us, died easy
one cold late November. In his sleep.

We kept the house I was born in,
rambling big rooms, the ways the dead stay on
in the scents of fireplaces and old furniture,
a worn feel to all the corners.
Like everyone, we sold the big acreage,
saving the pecan orchard, the peaches.
And we kept the life, somewhat: our garden,
a few horses, and a goat.

But some days, maybe in the middle of church
when Presbyterian voices
drag those hymns as if for bodies,
or in the middle of a class of seniors, or a row
of beans or stitches, papers to grade,
grandchildren, or petunias, I'll feel a shade
creep over me, a loneliness
so deep and strange it is like travel
without hope of home. And I'm overcome
with a wish so strong I jump,
thinking I've spoken.
Then, like the women in those harvest paintings,
I am *woman with a basket,* eyes distracted,
face turning away. And the basket overflowing,
and all the landscape golden and bereft.

That's when I reach toward what is not
there, this woman in the shut room of a city
who writes with a wall of books behind her,
writes this reaching toward the woman who is not
here, whose strong hands drop as she stops work to lose
all touch, standing in the yard in wonder at such sadness
that she never did see Greece or take the time
to think the way she knew she could, or write things down.
She had meant to do that, meant to write.
Oh what was it she had meant to write?

Now two women wake. Let's say they do.
Or one wakes and one cannot,

but which is not yet known. Two wake
in places that may or may not be real.
Their hands are warm and different and still.
They're blinking, startled as two children.
Neither can imagine where the daydream
came from, how it so absorbed her
it might have been
a depth-charged sleeping dream,
the kind you live in every muscle before dawn.

TO A YOUNG FEMINIST WHO
WANTS TO BE FREE

You describe your grandmothers walking straight
off the boats from Finland, Latvia
too late, early in this century, to bear blame
for sins we're bound to expiate:
in their funny hats, a potato in each pocket,
what possible American shame
could they hand down to me? You have your own
angers, you say. So much for the nineteenth
century's slavery, lynchings, native massacre, and the teeth
of cities still gnawing off the feet of survivors,
those gigantic traps still set.
You blame the men and free yourself of time
and fathers, displaced from more
than countries lost. Or never claimed.

I can't help thinking of the miserably hot summer
I taught in Michigan, where a July Fourth
was the whole *treasury of virtue* hammered home
in speeches praising Michigan and the lever of the war
that undid slavery and joined the union back.
Yet that whole campus was the record of a severing:
not one face in any class was black.
And only a few miles distant, our Detroit
was roiling and afire.
The students laughed at my slow southern accent,
joked that I'd brought the unaccustomed heat.

Perhaps I know too much, living as I must
with the lives (in letters) of great- and twice-great-
grandmothers,
southern women talking about their slaves
as if it were ordinary. It was. Sometimes the wills are there:
whole black families listed with the mules. It's terrible enough
to die about, and people did: the saviors and the guilty

and the simple poor. Never believe it's gone.
The stain is mine and I can't pass it anywhere but on,
and to my own. I live with what the past will not stop
proffering. I think it makes me wiser than you are,
who measure by the careful inch your accident
of time here and your innocence.
It lets you be only the victim,
lets you find the gold-
eyed goat still waiting in the bushes
to be bled.

Anyone who came here anytime
came here to take this country's gifts.
Not even you may refuse this one:
what's built on darkness rests on it.
And there is wisdom yet, though hard to see
in this peculiar light. It is the only light
we've got. And when was it *not* the case
(except in hell) that land and history
wear another's face?
Here is the necessary, fearsome, precious,
backward whole embrace.

POEM FOR DIZZY

written after discovering that no poem in *The Anthology of Jazz Poetry* is written to, for, or about Dizzy Gillespie, who was cocreator (with Charlie Parker) of bebop, the style that ushered in the modern jazz era

Sweet and sly, you were all business when the old bent-
skyward horn went up. Sometimes it went up like a rocket,
sometimes like a gentle-turning lark
high on a summer day. It could blow an island wind
snapping a line of red and yellow clothes
hard against blue.
The breath pouring into that banged-up
brass inclination heavenward
gave us lesson number one: *Be.*
Lesson number two came naturally.

And you were serious as sunrise. Those who scoffed
or bristled at the little stageside dance,
the cutting-up, the jokes and jive, have all gone off
to other targets. And you, Dizzy,
you've gone off too, asleep in your chair,
leaving us bereft. There was nobody better.

But there were lives the poets would want more—
for tragedy or politics, harsher
experiments: Bird's drugged vortex into *gone,*
Coltrane's absolute, Monk's edgy monologues, the demon
Miles Davis posed as, then became.
But you played clown, put everybody on.
You played the house, but played a soul into the horn.
And you outlived them all. This too was real jazz.

Talking, you were evasive, slant as a riff
around a melody, more private maybe
than anybody knew. I remember your one week

in our town, 1970:
afternoons you'd wander with your camera.
Putting his flute back in its case, Moody told us:
He does that every place we go, walks around
for hours by himself, just taking pictures
of wherever it is he is. Lesson number one.

You looked like the face of South Wind
in my childhood picture book,
like the best cherub
Italy ever chiseled above a doge
or saint, rich man, or pope.
What were you storing in those blown-out cheeks
all the years? Your darkest jokes?
some brand-new pure invention, notes
outside our hearing? Or perhaps some simple tune
we'd never have made much sense of,
the one about hope. The one about oldest love.

TIME AFTER TIME

*An Australian sound engineer has
developed a unique way of clearing the
hiss and clatter out of vintage jazz
recordings.*
   —Associated Press

Time: it does things
out there among the galaxies.
Clatter and hiss? Perhaps.
That's one metaphor for distance,

which is time. And our remembering?
There's less and less,
the dissonance of *now* and *then*
no longer audible when
mechanics cancels difference.

So out with the scritch of decades,
the sizzle and scar of error,
remembrance's waver, susurrus
of mortality, dust-riff, blues-ether.

We will turn *them* into *us*,
our sound loud as a spotlight,
bright as an electronic toy,
cleansed of those troublesome sixty years
and that old distortion: joy.

AT THE AGE WHEN YOU GET
BAD NEWS

Letting go of the future
is like this: trying to fit
back into the camera's aperture
before it closed that little square of time.
In this snapshot, I am fifteen,
all opening before me. I squint hard
against such brightness; perhaps I feared
the shutter's snicker.

Memory adds to what's outside the frame—
that fence, all rough-barked wood,
where my grandfather hung the dead
rattlesnake that wouldn't stay dead.
That fence, and the field beyond it
overgrown, one slightly agitated cow
heading for a shade tree.

But all that's beyond the picture's reach.
Here I am, feckless and posing.
My father stands beside me with his stick.
He's looking down so there's no face to him,
just hat with the brim turned down.
I'm wearing the sweater of pale lavender
that seemed made for someone prettier,
like the deep purple skirt
of corduroy soft as velvet.
It's all gray in this black-and-white,
the colors I'll get where I'm going.

In the picture I'm sitting on my heels
hugging the cur named Red
my father kept for squirrels,
and some of those in the out-of-focus trees
making the big dog's head begin its easy

swing toward joy, just as I am turning already
toward the path to this day two thousand miles away
that has brought me another death
and this kind of travel—
I do manage to get there before the picture,
where it's darker than it ever gets
until you've traveled afterward yourself.
Nobody's looked yet through the finder,
the lens not set, boundaries of white
paper not yet interrupting a translated sun.
I don't know what's going to happen
all over again at the speed of light:
the trees, my father, the blank sweater,
that dog starting to run.

EAST TEXAS AUTUMN AS A WAY TO SEE TIME

After the coded messages of wild geese are over,
misinterpreted as merely weather,
and after a few sharp nights have dipped
starpoint by starpoint to unstitch
the green from the meadows—
                              but before
the first chainlinks of ice have shut
the wings of twilight fiddlers and the gate
of the spider's vacant wheelhouse—
                              here's November
again, turned hot and sucking a groundfog.

It bears the bodies of my people, all given
to disappearing so suddenly in this season
the dirt had them before the wind could change.
By poisoned blood, locked heart, bad lungs, by bullet,
they were plunged deep where the year darkened
just *here*.
            As if there were a rule about it.

I've been gone so long I had forgotten
how a docile chill will just graze
the edges of morning and evening
holding between them a pillowful
of bright feathers, a trembling
of the thinnest wishbones passing tuneful
through this country, disassembling overhead
another summer.
                I could misremember
where the anniversaries are,
now that the downed, quilt-bright
leaves are soft underfoot,
though the trees are still ringing with color.
Here the ground lets the wet go,

suspiration of old rain climbing
visibly skyward in fog-rags.
                           A cold breath intaken.

By noon, alarum of sumac, boom
of red oak and maple, the ample light
cracking its whip, the holler of yellow
ditch-flowers, and every elbowing creek
a tributary to the old story of long lost
who never will come home—
down to the last chirper under
a dead bitterweed:
                           never, never.
It might as well be military,
the nights speaking skeletal sermons
windy as any general's.
                           And now,
now is the falling
forgetful under the last spell of lowland heat
turning over its brass to the brown earth victor.

Guessed at in the vaporous, piney margins,
the fugitive, brave impostor,
the season caught out of uniform,
caught out as a girl,
a girl, a dancer captured
in her own sweet turn. Almost
this minute she is quickest, loud-lit
with the cymbals of sundown—but not quite
yet and not for long and not likely
to leave more than a tatter of crimson
costume on the barbed-wire fence that is vanishing
over the softened hills, the little valleys
whose cattle are up to their knees in mist,
the still warm, silvered breath of this world
not quite undone.

Squint awhile. The distant fenceposts seem to move, become
a line of stragglers lost out of battle and gone

west, oh west, to tell
over the one campfire and ashes of dawn
November's tale: the bell in the blood,
the bright maps of birds, the world unhooded
in gunmetal light.
                    How nobody won.

IN A TRUNK NOT LOOKED INTO
FOR TWENTY YEARS

Snapshots curled in rigor mortis,
cuff links with the emblems of a lodge,
braided hair rings, a whistle, marbles,
hodgepodge of pocket knives, tin tops . . .
and here, Father, is that ringbox
I'd forgotten—in your faded
handwriting three words: *Redbud. Dark red.*

The box holds two small seeds
shining like brown taffeta.

Here in my hand is your shy love for color.
The painter you might have been spoke once
when you told us all the story of a doll
you saw as a boy at a carnival—
how you loved her dress of scarlet silk,
how it shone still on barbs of memory.
You were thirteen, a crack shot.
And you won. No one laughed
at the uneasy prize you chose:
to hold that bright material awhile
before your delighted sisters got the doll.

Flowers you'd bring from hunting trips
would be as dead before you got them home
as any meat you'd shot—
wild orchids we didn't know were rare,
carnivorous sundew, bluebonnets
too blue, bogflowers nameless and scarce.
Sometimes you'd have a branch of redbud
wilting beside you in the truck.
You said it kept the winter back.

Dark red. You'd found a strange one,
deeper colored, extraordinary. You marked the place

and you came back in autumn for the seeds.
You thought I'd want to raise
in my suburban backyard a thing uncanny
as your wilderness kept turning out to be,
where creek banks sown with the teeth of ancient seas
bloomed with furred and pliant shadows,
where the green air turned and turned
its whirligig of birds.

When I was a child, you sketched them all for me,
each creature in its chosen place,
even the serpent curled on a branch, asleep.
I have the pencil drawings still,
bleached but full of detail, primitive
and skilled and wary as the animals themselves
printing their tracks on that preyed-over ground.

Now I've just returned from another country—
the whole Peloponnese was snared in bloom.
At Olympia, the broken columns lay
in a shoal of Judas trees,
the hold of Zeus ashimmer in pink fire.
Redbud. Judas tree. The same
branches of such ill luck they had to bear
the awful dead weight of remorse.
Greek blossoms surged like fountains
among the shattered temples, betrayal everywhere.

I've heard of seeds taken from a tomb
in Egypt, planted in sterile soil, and brought to bloom.
Not here, Father. Nothing's here
but this inheritance: my imagining eye
sketching on a windowpane the strange
vision of a tree like a scarlet skirt
afire among ghosts of the shrinking forest,
suddenly bright
as the spreading blossom of blood you lost,
and desperate with spring.

WRITING POEMS LATE

The summer's little clocks, soft works awhir,
are loose among the darkening trees, weighting the air
exactly as they did that year when death
turned suddenly original—

and here I stop
as surely as a summer's voices thin
to sere and silence in the closing hand of cold.
Already it is a kind of winter, this ice on the tongue.
If I were a bird, I'd be the wrong one. A toad
is more appropriate for any ode we'd have:
it sleeps and waits
to make its ugly revolution in
the glass-jar air of what we'll take for spring.

If I speak of a porch light that still casts,
somewhere, that peculiar deepened yellow glow
you'd seen on summer nights against the leaning house?
That's only sepia the memory layers over
what will print but cannot last,
like shadow in its clockwise march.
The scene I won't flesh into words could make me weep—

and that is disallowed, of course, unless
for grief addressable, a present tense
quite shadowless and pure:
The World as System or *Language as a City*—
the critics, agile as paramecia, play
under a sun renewed, always renewed—
The Ideological Gesture, Historical Overdetermination,
The Absence of a Transcendental Signified,
and *Authenticity, Meditations on.*

Meantime there is this old demanding
repetition: memory thick as evening in the trees,

the pool of yellow porchlight full of wings
beyond which the first real dark has come
in a metallic skirl, a din
as of icebergs touching in another world.

ARGUMENT

*There's no real difference between a spear and a
nuclear rocket. Both are just technology, and I
shouldn't like being killed by a spear any more
than by an intercontinental missile. What I'm
saying is, a death's a death; it comes to the same
thing.*
          —the Younger Poet at dinner

I can't deny you know much more
about some worlds that I can know.
You've studied physics.
Your poems are exquisite with learning.

And I hadn't thought I'd been here long enough
to be some part of an older generation,
having no wisdom but only a skulking
certainty that might actually be furred—

or not far from it. Something truly old
rises in me at what you've said,
something like smoke and a shadow unfolding
at the edge of an interior fire.

How to answer, young friend,
your sure equation? A spear
is attached to a specific hand and eye
until the last fraction of a minute:

my argument's in that,
and in the skill of the individual
who determines the whole of this act,
including the audible cracking of bone,

the breath going out, the screech
a soul makes leaving—

that bubble and prayer of death
immediate, tangible as the self.

Let's say it's almost a kind of justice
that the man who releases a spear
must watch the death he's made, if only
to retrieve the bloody spear.

This is not pleasant conversation,
but no one is talking about pleasure.
We are talking about man. A man.
A man who has thrown with utmost care

a spear. He has real blood on him;
even a gun will take away such obligation.
But this act is local and stays local
as when a wooden plow is used, an ax, an awl.

The definers say a plow's as much technology
as a computer is, meaning whatever works
in human hands. Whatever works.
But there is a dividing line not named

by the namers, a line glare-blue, drawn
by no hand we can remember, clear
as a cave painting in firelight.
Something like *bear*

stands up between the rocket and the spear.

SIPHNOS, 1987

I have seen the sun break through to illuminate a
small field for awhile, and gone my way and
forgotten it. But that was the pearl of great price, the
one field that had the treasure in it.
  —R. S. Thomas, "The Bright Field"

Just past our neighbors' lemon trees
heavy with their eggs of light,
one plot of ground was measured out
by stone walls whitewashed to shining—
something I might glance toward, walking on.
It was as blunt as any field in Wales,
as full of weather in a place where weather
likewise mints the farmer's coin.
But this piece of land was given over.

I'd never seen wild flowers in such riot:
empurpled, gilded, smeared with the blue of icons.
And wide-faced poppies crowded luminous
as figures in the stained glass of cathedrals,
the blood of saints in them.
I hadn't guessed Greek sunlight could repeat
at certain moments everything
that's been said about it—*molten*
gold, honey, wine—pouring overmuch
on April's prism, making rich
even the wooden donkey saddle waiting
daisy-bestridden beneath an almond tree.

In air so clear, any sound will carry
until it seems almost material
beneath a sky that holds its clarity
the way St. Spirodon's blue dome
above the dark chants holds perfection.
A fisherman in the village square was calling

the names of his catch, red mullet
leaping in his voice. The priest's donkey
clattered past in a stutter of yellow.
Behind the stone church, a woman
in a moan of black skirts combed
her child's hair softly with a song
green as the turning sea.
And surely the ragged wail sent down
by the goat lost on the mountain
bore the violet bruises of despair.

I stayed the morning there, in thrall
to something in particular.
Memory has taken it: white wall, the shine
of voices, the blossoms plying like gaudy fish
their sea of wind.
This was the bright field, the burning bush
that startles stone to words. It outstays
Mycenae's gate, Delphi's high and sibilant ruin;
the laws already broken
of matter and of time.

Notes

1. "Intervale": The word *intervale* is an obsolete form of *interval.* In parts of the U.S. the older term survived to mean a stretch of low land next to a river. The old word contains the new—I wanted all the meanings, especially the modern usage of interval that refers to the difference in pitch between two musical sounds, either successive (in melody) or in harmony. The more ordinary meaning of interval—a time or space between—is also useful for the poem and this book.

Italicized first lines of stanzas in the "Bass," "Treble," "Tenor," and "Counter" sections of the poem are direct quotations from hymns in *The Sacred Harp Songbook,* revised by W. M. Cooper and published in Dothan, Alabama, in 1902.

Distinctive traits of Sacred Harp music include chords with the middle tone missing, parallel fifths, and parallel octaves. Often fugal, the songs are harmonized on separate staves for each part. The unusual notation is a representation of syllables of the scale ("fa-sol-la") by geometric shapes. Hymns are first sung through, using only these syllables, before the words are sung. Unaccompanied, made by the whole congregation rather than a choir, the music is driven by a powerful surging beat and frequently uses uncommon modal scales.

The "Interlude" section is taken almost verbatim from interviews with my mother's siblings and others who knew her.

2. "Cycladic Figure": The people who inhabited the Cycladic islands of Greece for over a thousand years beginning in 2600 B.C. left no trace except for their simple tombs. Buried in the tombs were large numbers of marble idols that have been called "elegant" and "sophisticated." Usually female, they have an angular, abstract shape and a disciplined refinement beyond the primitive. Based on the small statue in the North Carolina Museum of Art (see cover photograph), the poem uses this bare image as metaphor for an interval between the human fall from animal being into thought, and the later complications of advanced civilizations.

3. "Untitled Triptych": The poem suggests competing but finally reconciled interpretations of the North Carolina Museum of Art's powerful triptych by Anselm Kiefer. Born in Berlin in 1945, Kiefer is part of the generation of German artists whose work has dealt with the burden of German history. The painting measures nearly eleven feet high by more than eighteen feet wide. The poem's first two sections deal with the left and right panels; the third section confronts the center panel, the problematic but reconciling figures of ladder and serpent.

Uncompromising and dense, the Kiefer creates a complex, opaque, and unforgettable material experience. It contains surprising subtleties of color, wide ranges of grays and browns, dim and brightening blues, and a tawny yellow moving to gold in certain light, the whole paradoxically enlivened and made darker by glints of actual lead fragments embedded in the paint. The boulders in the left panel are actual large stones dipped in lead and held by steel cables. The center ladder is cast metal suspended from a jutting rod. The protuberance at the bottom corner of the right panel seems a burnt, fleshy flower, or a ghostly loudspeaker emerging from the canvas. Straw and ashes added to layers of paint create a sense of fragility and desolation in this massive work. The piece dreams our twentieth-century nightmare, its inner and its outer existence. The artist layered the painting on top of a vastly enlarged landscape photograph. The triptych is unrelenting yet seems to hint at possible redemption, if only through art.

4. "The Swan Story": the poem loosely follows the plot of Hans Christian Andersen's fairy tale "The Wild Swans," recast here as interior autobiography. The poem's speaker takes all the parts, the enchanted brothers' as well as that of the sister who must try to undo the spell. I have made the tale an

extended metaphor for a young girl's growing up, told by her as an adult to her husband as they walk in the snow. "Bird-Loose-Feather" in the last line is the English translation of the Old Norse word for snow. The brother who is left with a swan's wing (and who is part of the speaker's interior life) can be seen as the poet's earthbound flying.